[Citation Needed] 2: The Needening

To Nathan, my Favorite
local artist — enjoy the
art of wikipedia ~~jokes~~
jokes! (This is a lost
art Firm.)

John F~~

[Citation Needed] 2: The Needening

More Of
The Best of Wikipedia's Worst Writing

Conor Lastowka and Josh Fruhlinger

Boring Legal Fine Print

Copyediting by Lauren Lastowka
Cover design by Jaime Robinson

ISBN # 978-1484909126

*Dedicated to the guy who won
the 40,000-word edit war over the
capitalization of "Star Trek Into Darkness"*

Foreword

The Information Age—what vast and manifold wonders it has brought! The instant interconnectivity of billions of human minds; endless stores of the accumulated wisdom of Man such as the creators of the Great Library of Alexandria could only dream; and more videos of goats yelling like people than one person could watch in ten lifetimes!

If your great-great-grandfather wanted to hear a goat yell like a person (if he didn't he was crazy) he'd have to take time off from his job at the mustache wax factory, climb the ladder to the seat of his velocipede, realize that his legs didn't reach the pedals, pitch violently while attempting to dismount, fall off, hitting his head on steps ten, eight, and four of the ladder on his way down, damaging his bowler hat in the process, and landing himself in the hospital. When he got there, as was common at the time, the goat who yells like a person would be his attending nurse. Then it was but a small matter to ask for a glass of water and the yelling would begin.

But goat videos aside, the greatest invention of the Information Age is perhaps Wikipedia. (I say "perhaps" because among experts there is disagreement. Some say it most certainly isn't while others, if you suggest it, simply laugh and flick lit cigarettes at your head.) Still its significance is huge: a dictionary to which anyone can add their knowledge! Imagine it—a vast body of scholars from diverse backgrounds and disciplines rounding out and expanding our understanding of, say, the Reformation, its milieu, its causes, its effects, the profound ways in which it has shaped even our present times!

Now that you've imagined it, go ahead and immediately forget it, also taking a moment to feel stupid for falling for my suggestion in the first place, 'cause it ain't gonna happen. However, if you are sick of chasing down long-dead Geocities sites hoping to find out which season it was of "The A-Team" where they started blacking out the GMC logo on the front of the van and wanted that information in one tidy place, then Wikipedia is a godsend.

Or say you are writing a term paper on The Significance of Cryptograms in the Program Works of Robert Schumann and need some information on his Carnaval op. 9. Well, put that aside for the time being. Writing term papers is too hard. Instead why not crack open a Bud Chelada, head over to Wikipedia, pull up the entry for the My Buddy doll and delve into the controversy over whether it was it or the "That Kid" doll that served as inspiration for Chucky from the Child's Play franchise! (It was the "That Kid" doll and if you say otherwise then die in a fire.)

As Josh and Conor so entertainingly highlighted at their blog and in volume one of Citation Needed, Wikipedia's approach is something of a variation on the "infinite monkeys" theory that might be stated thusly: If you open up the editing of your encyclopedia to a nearly infinite amount of people, sooner or later you are going to get some very bad, confused, and often very funny entries.

At great personal risk they have trawled the backwaters of Jimmy Wales's river of crowdsourced knowledge, have pored over entries almost certainly unread since the time of their creation (possibly not even at the time of their creation), have for your entertainment and delight fact-checked every word of the article on the Country Bear Christmas Special. (Rid yourself of that nagging doubt that perhaps they stumbled upon it while looking for information on that girl bear with the long eyelashes, the tutu, and the big blue bow on her head. Please. This is science.)

Besides the commentaries from your editors (in italics) the entries have not been altered in any way but represent (or did at the time) Wikipedia's Official and Royal Last Word on the Subject.

I hope you enjoy this tour of Wikipedia's worst writing as much as I did!

—Michael J. Nelson

P.S. The girl bear's name is Trixie.

"He who controls the past controls the future. He who controls the present controls the past."
—George Orwell, Nineteen Eighty-Four

"The episode "The God Complex" of Doctor Who should be put in similar works beacuse in the episode, they are in the hotel where each room contains someone's greatest fear."
—Wikipedia talk page for Ninteen Eighty-Four

Citation

A prime purpose of a citation is intellectual honesty[citation needed]

> Ah yes, "Intellectual honesty." A firm pillar that Wikipedia is established upon. Keep this in mind one hundred pages from now when you are reading about the regional variations of the "blow job gesture."

http://en.wikipedia.org/wiki/Citation

Glasgow Ice Cream Wars

The conflicts, in which vendors raided one another's vans and fired shotguns into one another's windscreens, were more violent than might typically be expected between ice-cream salesmen.

And yet, since nobody was left to die in agony in an alleyway bleeding from a stab wound to the kidney, the conflicts were considerably less violent than might typically be expected between Scotsmen.

http://en.wikipedia.org/wiki/Glasgow_Ice_Cream_Wars

F.A.R.T. the Movie

Russell is obsessed with farting, and loves to fart any time he can. His girlfriend, Heather despises farts and becomes angry with Russell because all he does is watch television and fart. She tells him that the only time she can feel relaxed is when Russell is out of the house, as she is away from his gas. She thinks that if the television turns into fart jokes, which he also loves, then Russell won't even leave the house. Then one night, the television does become all about farts. This puts Heather to the ultimate test to see if she can get past his problem and love him. In the end, she has become so fed up with farting that she has a nightmare about farting. She wakes up and Russell farts. Heather realizes that there is no point in hating it anymore and decides to love him. The film concludes with both of them farting gleefully.

Critics called it "a baffling change of pace" for director Steven Spielberg, with many of them questioning whether it was the most suitable project for the acclaimed director to follow-up Schindler's List with.

http://en.wikipedia.org/wiki/F.A.R.T._the_Movie

List of retronyms

Before canned corn was widely available, "corn on the cob" was simply "corn."

An excerpt from the popular book 101 Facts To Elicit a Disdainful Sigh From Your Texting Grandchild.

Sgt. Pepper's Lonely Hearts Club Band

Adolf Hitler, Mahatma Gandhi and Jesus Christ were requested by Lennon, but ultimately they were left out. Except for Ghandi who does appear on the cover of the first issued albums. He was placed under a Palm tree, so he would not be too visible. He was later removed.

Go fuck yourself, concept of coherent thought!

http://en.wikipedia.org/wiki/Sgt._Pepper%27s_Lonely_Hearts_Club_Band

Turnover (food)

The turnovers will also bear the term "turnover" on the product's label; if the label does not identify the product as "turnover," the product is most likely not a turnover.

A shadowy figure in a trench coat grows nervous as the rube he is about to unload three tons of unlabeled black market "turnovers" on decides to check Wikipedia before sealing the deal.

http://en.wikipedia.org/wiki/Turnover_(food)

Southern Comfort

Janis Joplin is mediumly associated with this beverage.[citation needed]

The author of this article is mediumly fluent in the English language.

Sod's Law

Adolph Coors III, who was allergic to beer, was the heir to the Coors beer empire—being allergic to beer is bad fortune for many, but it is Sod's Law that someone allergic to beer would inherit a beer empire (and, due to a botched kidnapping attempt, die because of the empire's wealth, thus being killed by beer, if only indirectly).

No doubt he died with a chuckle on his lips, recognizing the irony. Or maybe he died in a state of mortal terror, begging for his life? Ugh, no, we like the first one better.

http://en.wikipedia.org/wiki/Sod's_law

House of Sand and Fog (film)

Fog plays a major role in the film; Sand, not as much.

"Four stars." —Anakin Skywalker

http://en.wikipedia.org/wiki/House_of_Sand_and_Fog_(film)

Unibrow

Unibrow color is not affected by the dying of one's hair; unless one were to dye the unibrow as well.

File this one under "Grooming tips guys read a few hours before being rejected."

http://en.wikipedia.org/wiki/Unibrow

2008

According to the Futurama episode "Space Pilot 3000", Stop 'N Drop suicide booths are claimed to have been "America's Favorite" since 2008. Whether this is the use of an advertising hyperbole to indicate that they were introduced in 2008, or that they gained a plurality of market share in 2008 is not concluded.

Market share seems like a crude metric for deeming a service "America's favorite," but it's difficult to rate the customer satisfaction levels for a chain of suicide booths, for obvious reasons. Anyway, writers of cartoon shows should probably give a little thought to this stuff before each and every throwaway joke they write.

http://en.wikipedia.org/wiki/2008

Godzilla Raids Again

Anguirus hated Godzilla, which explains the intense rivalry between the two monsters.

For many Zen novices, their first true test comes when they first encounter the kōan, "Which came first, Anguirus's hatred of Godzilla or the intense rivalry between Anguirus and Godzilla?"

The answer actually turns out to be: C) That time Godzilla banged Anguirus's wife.

http://en.wikipedia.org/wiki/Godzilla_Raids_Again

East Germany jokes

What was the most-frequently used word at the German-German border? "Goose meat". (Gänsefleisch, sounds like the first three words in Gönn'se vielleischt mal 'n Gofferraum bidde offmachn? in the Saxon accent, Können Sie vielleicht bitte mal den Kofferraum öffnen? in standard German, which means Could you please open the trunk?) This joke cannot be fully understood unless one realizes that most East German border guards who worked at the West German border were recruited from Saxony, the most populous part of the country and larger parts thereof without availability of West German broadcasts.[citation needed]

> "And what's the deal with the food at Stasi internment camps? We've all been there, right? Suspected of betraying the People's Revolution, tortured within an inch of our lives until we accuse all our closest friends of terrible crimes they didn't commit, just to make it stop? Right? This is my 'relatable' material. Hello? Is this thing on?"

http://en.wikipedia.org/wiki/East_Germany_jokes

Double entendre

An example might be if one were to say "It's too big to fit in my mouth" upon being served a large sandwich, someone else could say "That's what she said," as if the statement were a reference to oral sex.

http://en.wikipedia.org/wiki/Double_entendre

On the Air (TV series)

Blinky Watts (Tracey Walter) - master sound effects technician for "The Lester Guy Show". He suffers from "Bozeman's Simplex," a disease that causes him to see 25.62 times more than everyone else. It comes off oven mitt. Oven mitt. Oven mitt. We are frequently reminded that Blinky is not blind but sees more, because the show takes place in 1957 and his best friend is black, this shows the viewer that Blinky is not racist but could be if he wanted.

Guys, is it possible for a Wikipedia article to have a stroke?

http://en.wikipedia.org/wiki/On_the_Air_(TV_series)

John Other Day

In recognition of his service, Congress granted him recognition for his services.

> *Jay Leno put down his newspaper. "Sheila, have the entire writing staff clear their schedules," he said into his intercom. This would be his finest hour.*

http://en.wikipedia.org/wiki/John_Other_Day

Disney Princess

Unofficial princesses

Kiara - Although the daughter of Simba in The Lion King 2 is technically a princess, Disney does not consider her one for the reason that she is a Lion.

Also, lions are not permitted to enter the Disneyland or Disney World resorts, nor are they permitted to book rooms at Disney-branded hotels or buy passage on Disney cruise ships. The sad but unavoidable conclusion: Disney is racist against lions.

http://en.wikipedia.org/wiki/Disney_Princess

List of Sabrina, the Teenage Witch characters

Kenan and Kel appeared in their house where Kenan was looking for the lottery ticket while Kel is making a sandwich and Kenan finds it and accidentally puts it in the sandwich that Kel was making and runs and says that he found the ticket, Kel comes back in the kitchen not realizing that the ticket is in the sandwich he made and puts the remaining ingredients he was going to put on plus the other bread and starts eating the sandwich, Kenan comes back and sees that Kel is eating the sandwich and he got sad.

Welcome to BuzzFeed's newest web series, "Glenn Danzig reads Wikipedia synopses of Kenan & Kel scenes out loud."

(We would actually watch this.)

Found Art

Trash art may also have a social purpose, of raising awareness of trash.

The author of this entry would like to remind you that an incredibly stupid social purpose is still technically a social purpose.

Beethoven's 2nd

Ryce attends a party with friends where she is exposed to vices of teen culture such as binge drinking and getting locked in her former boyfriend's bedroom against her will.

Charles Grodin's young daughter is imprisoned by a former lover. The corrupting stink of substance abuse oozes out of the walls of her cell. Sexual assault seems imminent; her virginity will not be hers much longer. Fortunately Charles has a very particular set of skills; skills he has acquired over a very longUH-OH! BEETHOVEN'S EATING THE TURKEY OFF THE TABLE AND THE BOSS IS COMING OVER FOR DINNER IN ... FIFTEEN MINUTES??? WHO'S GOING TO CLEAN UP ALL THAT SLOBBER?

Air rage

Other related behavior that may interfere with the comfort of cabin crew or passengers include smoking on board the flight, viewing pornographic materials, performing sex acts ("mile high" club) in the aircraft cabin, making undue sexual advances towards other people, performing sex acts in the lavatory, the inappropriate groping and touching of crew members, loud or drunken behaviors, spitting, swearing, and wearing clothing that is inappropriate or offensive.

A plaque honoring the time Bill Clinton "hit for the cycle" by accomplishing all of these in one flight is proudly displayed in the lavatory of Air Force One.

Sword in the Stone (attraction)

Sword in the Stone is a world of attractions in the Disney parks. The attraction is based on the Disney's Sword in the Stone.

The film was the motif of attraction. Even though attraction, only has a sword stuck in the rocks. This is the film "Sword in the Stone" and its origin is "The Story of King Arthur" episode comes out, ie, is pulled out with a rock stuck in Seiken Densetsu becomes King of Britain (Excalibur), a is reproduced. Incidentally, the story of King Arthur is the story go from where we pulled out the sword, in the original movie is "King of eternity," the first part of (ends at Arthur pulled the sword), the film only because it ends at the king deemed legitimate, pull out the sword.

This attraction is Merlin the magician performances of the equipment. Guests may pull out sword in the performances.

This attraction's description was written by someone who just spent twelve hours sweating inside the Goofy suit on a 101-degree Orlando day.

Reseda, Los Angeles

The Sav On, previously mentioned (it was actually there in the 1950s) was where we kids would go to stock up on candy, three candy bars for a quarter, before the start of the movie.

Also, next door, was a donut shop with a giant donut on top. In a tragic move, that giant donut was torn down when a corner gas station replaced the donut shop.

Welcome to the crowdsourced future, everyone! Who needs "professional historians" when you have old people rambling on the internet about the places where they grew up?

http://en.wikipedia.org/wiki/Reseda,_Los_Angeles

Pinky swear

It is also possible for a pinky swear to exist between 3 parties, known as a 3-way pinky promise. A pinky swear between 4 or more people is relatively unknown.

A pinky swear involving five or more people is known as a "pinky rat king" and has been rumored to snap off of the hands of the swearers and skitter horribly across the floor.

http://en.wikipedia.org/wiki/Pinky_swear

Cheese sandwich

A cheese sandwich is a basic sandwich made generally with one or more slices of any kind of cheese on any sort of bread.

From the Food Network's newest hit series Anthony Bourdain Phones It In.

http://en.wikipedia.org/wiki/Cheese_sandwich

Martin Soap

Soap tries to arrest the Punisher, but fails to stop him. Soap then becomes despondent; Castle then tells Soap when things aren't getting better, to "just go".

Soap leaves the NYPD, moves to Los Angeles and becomes a porn star. Up to that point, he had simply been unaware that he has large genitals.

Are you one of the 97% of readers that surreptitiously glanced down at your own genitals before moving on to this comment? You know, just in case you too had been unaware? How'd that work out for you?

http://en.wikipedia.org/wiki/Martin_Soap

Richie Ramone

Richie did a very lovely thing by attending Joey Ramone's funeral on April 17, 2001, two days after Joey passed away. Ramones creative director, Arturo Vega commented of this in a nice way on Richie Ramone turned up after a two-decade absence to speak for the animals, was written in first press release text of Richie in December, 2005.

> *The animals were so touched by Richie turning up to speak for them that one, undeterred by its lack of opposable thumbs or a grasp of the concept of language, logged on to Wikipedia to edit some compliments into his page.*

Phlegm

Coughing up any significant quantity of blood is always a serious medical condition, and any person who experiences this should seek medical attention.[citation needed]

It's a mystery why advocates for health care reform in the United States ignore high-tech disruptive innovations like Wikipedia-based diagnostics.

http://en.wikipedia.org/wiki/Phlegm

Childhood secret club

Pro forma secrecy. The secrecy may be more imaginary than real. For instance the name of the club and its membership are usually obvious to all. There may be a desire to create secret codes and plans, but they are rarely implemented. A ramshackle den, tree house, clubhouse, fort, or "secret base" may be built in nearby scrub-land or an abandoned building.

Other good ideas for locations for your Secret Kids Club HQ: A vacant lot strewn with glass, the blood-stained basement of an abandoned mental hospital, an uncleared minefield in a jungle where a long-forgotten war was fought, the floor-to-ceiling-carpeted back of the trademark white van of an overly friendly local drifter...

Country Bear Christmas Special

At Disney Word, the Christmas Special ran until 2005 due to copyrights w/ some songs in the show like Rudolph the Red-Nosed Reindeer. But is rumored to return in the future!

You've just encountered the most depressing exclamation point in the history of the English language.

http://en.wikipedia.org/wiki/Country_Bear_Christmas_Special

Center, Kentucky

The mayor of center is Marty Pennington a very well respected man and his son Austin well lets just say hes took after his father.

> *"Austin, get the hell off of Wikipedia! Your dad is cutting the ribbon at the new Applebee's in fifteen minutes!"*

http://en.wikipedia.org/wiki/Center,_Kentucky

Urban warfare

The British military terms are OBUA (operations in built-up areas), FIBUA (fighting in built-up areas), or sometimes (colloquially) FISH (fighting in someone's house), or FISH and CHIPS (fighting in someone's house and causing havoc in people's streets). A lesser known term is used by the S.A.S. for their specialist first strike and reconnaissance team, known as FART (First Assault Reconnaissance Team).[citation needed]

> *The British are far too classy to make any kind of "silent but deadly joke," so we guess we'll refrain... Oh, wait, Benny Hill was British, wasn't he? Never mind. [series of flatulence noises]*

Diary of a Cannibal

Something about Adam isn't quite right, though, when he insists that Noelle eat him in order for them to be "truly one."

Ooh, ooh, let us guess: What isn't quite right about him is ... he wears sandals with socks? He breathes really loud through his nose? He prefers the clearly inferior direct-to-video sequel An Extremely Goofy Movie *to the original* A Goofy Movie?

Are we close?

http://en.wikipedia.org/wiki/Diary_of_a_Cannibal

Moo box

The Moo box is a box, when you turn it upside down, creates the mooing of a cow.

How's this for a bleak realization: It's extremely unlikely that your life will ever be notable enough to warrant its own Wikipedia entry. Unlike the Moo box.

http://en.wikipedia.org/wiki/Moo_box

Batusi

The Batusi is performed by making a horizontal V-sign with one's index and middle fingers of both hands, and drawing them across in front of the eyes, one hand at a time, with the eyes roughly between the fingers. This is performed in time with the music, and is improved upon by continuing to dance with the lower half of the body, simultaneously.

Another method of improving the Batusi is to stop doing the Batusi immediately and go back and sit at the table in the corner with all the other people the bride and groom invited to the wedding out of a sense of obligation.

Sir Mix-a-lot

Despite having taken several years off from recording, Sir Mix-a-Lot is still known to mix frequently.

*Wait, so the "a-lot" in Sir Mix-a-Lot refers to his **frequency** of mixing, not the large amount of records that he mixes?? Wow... Wow...*

Excuse us, we need to lie down for a while. This ... This changes things.

http://en.wikipedia.org/wiki/Sir_Mix-a-Lot

Galaxian

The game's plot consists of a title screen that displayed the message "WE ARE THE GALAXIANS / MISSION: DESTROY ALIENS".

Michael Bay is in talks to adapt this plot into three horrible films beginning in 2015.

http://en.wikipedia.org/wiki/Galaxian

Victor Salva

Victor Ronald Salva (born March 29, 1958) is an American film director. He is best known for directing the films Powder and Jeepers Creepers, and his conviction for child molestation.

> *The fact that* Jeepers Creepers II *was left off this list of Salva's notable accomplishments in favor of "child molestation conviction" is more damning than any Rotten Tomatoes ranking could ever be.*

http://en.wikipedia.org/wiki/Victor_Salva

The Station nightclub fire

Five months after the fire, Great White started a benefit tour, saying a prayer at the beginning of each concert for the friends and families touched by that fateful night and giving a portion of the proceeds to the Station Family Fund. The band said they would never play the song "Desert Moon" again. "I don't think I could ever sing that song again," said lead singer and founder Jack Russell. Guitarist Mark Kendall stated, "We haven't played that song. Things that bring back memories of that night we try to stay away from. And that song reminds us of that night. We haven't played it since then and probably never will." The band has since resumed playing the song.

It's almost as if an '80s hair metal band had failed to invest the riches they earned in their transient heydey wisely, and were forced to play whatever their few remaining fans wanted to hear in order to squeeze the last few possible dollars from their legacy, even if doing so would fly in the face of their promises and basic human decency!

http://en.wikipedia.org/wiki/The_Station_nightclub_fire

Raffi (musician)

He has long been a firm believer in the beauty of children, and very open about expressing the firmness of his beliefs.[citation needed]

Reading about Raffi's firmness, we came to a horrifying realization: We could take either side of the argument "What is the best nickname for Raffi to have for his penis: Baby Beluga or Bananaphone?" and debate it for at least an hour while intoxicated.

Book of Thugs

Book of Thugs: Chapter AK Verse 47 is the third studio album by rapper Trick Daddy, two years afterwww.thug.com. It was released on February 15, 2000 byAtlantic Records and Slip-n-Slide Records. The album went gold. The name of the album subliminally states the automatic assault rifle, AK-47.

The artist behind songs such as "Suckin' Fuckin'," "Stroke it Gently," and "Kill Your Ass" is known for such subtlety.

http://en.wikipedia.org/wiki/Book_of_Thugs

Snow Miser

In the 1997 film Batman & Robin, Mr. Freeze (portrayed by Arnold Schwarzenegger) tries to teach his thugs the Snow Miser song, and it didn't work out too well.

"Didn't work out too well" is literally the most extravagant praise anyone has ever lavished on any aspect of this film.

http://en.wikipedia.org/wiki/Snow_Miser

Maurice Sendak

In terms of influencing others, Sendak has been a massive influence over the decades.

After years of being influential in the art of influencing, Sendak became a master of the little practiced art of Influenception. He nearly died attempting a third-level Influenception, in which he attempted to influence Roald Dahl to influence J.K. Rowling, only to realize that Shel Silverstein had subconsciously influenced him to perform the Influenception. This knowledge, and the new lease on life he was afforded after the resulting twenty-nine-day coma, influenced Sendak to write Where The Wild Things Are, *a book so influential that right about here is the point where the humble joke writer realized he was in over his head and decided to pull the plug on the entire bit.*

http://en.wikipedia.org/wiki/Maurice_Sendak

Snickerdoodle

Yet another hypothesis suggests that the name has no particular meaning or purpose and is simply a whimsically named cookie that originated from a New England tradition of fanciful cookie names.

If you ever need to explain to your children or grandchildren why it was so important that we invent movies, television, and the internet, you just tell them that there was a whole region of the country that used to sit around thinking up wacky names for cookies, for fun.

http://en.wikipedia.org/wiki/Snickerdoodle

Splinter (Teenage Mutant Ninja Turtles)

He was a martial art instructor for the Foot Clan, based in Japan, and also had a passion for Renaissance art. But he didn't talk very much though, for he was very quiet.

Splinter was a firm believer in the aphorism "It is better to remain silent and be thought a fool than to edit a Wikipedia article about a giant mutant rat martial arts instructor and remove all doubt."

http://en.wikipedia.org/wiki/Splinter_(Teenage_Mutant_Ninja_Turtles)

Disappointment

Modern-day and informal usage and expression of disappointment is sometimes used by saying "*Aww…*" This is usually followed by another phrase, such as "*that's too bad*" or "*better luck next time*". Different variations of this phrase vary from "*Aww, man…*" and "*Aw, shoot!*"

Below is an example of the usage of the above phrase:

"We lost the baseball game 3-5."
"Aww…"

Actual transcript of the conversation between A-Rod and his mom in the Yankees' clubhouse following the team's elimination from the 2012 postseason.

Mr. Magoo

Columbia was reluctant to release the short, but did so, only because it included a bear.

This decision was made during a brief period of time when a shadowy group of executives took over Columbia Pictures. Sporting silly hats and arriving at work every day via unicycle, they claimed to be "foreign investors." They kept mostly to themselves, but attempted to institute odd changes to the studio's culture. Break room coffee pots were replaced with bee hives dripping with sweet, sweet honey. A river was rerouted through the board room and stocked with wild salmon. A slight uptick in backlot maulings was reported.

It eventually turned out that they were Belgian, which surprised all the employees who had just assumed that they were a bunch of hyper-intelligent bears.

https://en.wikipedia.org/wiki/Mr._Magoo

Bébé's Kids

Producers of the film believe if the film featured cartoon dogs, it would've been more successful.

> *We can only imagine that the producers' heads would have exploded if the film contained a bear.*

http://en.wikipedia.org/wiki/B%C3%A9b%C3%A9%27s_Kids

Khalil Greene

He announced on February 22, 2010 that, suffering another episode of social anxiety disorder, he would not be reporting to Rangers spring training. On February 25, the Rangers voided Greene's contract.

Other interests
Greene writes hip-hop lyrics in his spare time and adds them to music. He is an adherent of the Bahá'í Faith, and says his faith has helped his athletic performance mentally.

Proponents of the Bahá'í Faith welcome the endorsement from Mr. Green, and kindly request that you ignore the first paragraph.

http://en.wikipedia.org/wiki/Khalil_Greene

Hugs and kisses

Some sources discuss the possibility of "x" referring to hugs and "o" referring to kisses. However, some sources indicate that "x" is used to signify a kiss and "o" is used to signify a hug.

One additional source has only ever received one letter in her life and instead of x's and o's, it just had a drawing of two dogs humping. This kind of made it easier, since it didn't matter which dog signified kisses and which dog signified hugs, but it was still off-putting coming from the office of former Speaker of the House Tip O'Neill.

Pin the Tail on the Donkey

Pin the Tail on the Donkey is suitable for children who are old enough to walk and to know better than to eat the small sharp tacks.

Kids who are dumb enough to eat sharp tacks may enjoy an alternative activity, such as "Just look at the tail and don't go anywhere near the donkey," "Find a corner and sit in it," "That's dog fur, where did you get that?," and "Here's a cardboard box, your mom will be here in an hour."

http://en.wikipedia.org/wiki/Pin_the_tail_on_the_donkey

David Allan Coe

After the Internal Revenue Service seized his home in Key West, Florida, Coe lived in a cave in Tennessee, and later remarried and got back on his feet.

Wikipedia: where the fascinating-sounding process of getting back on your feet by hiding from the IRS in a cave barely warrants a passing mention because the author had to go write two thousand words about a slight change in appearance of the uniform of one of the ThunderCats between seasons two and three.

http://en.wikipedia.org/wiki/David_Allan_Coe

Stacey Q

2.4 Post-1980s solo career
    2.4.1 One-hit wonder status
    2.4.2 Conversion to Buddhism

Laugh if you want, it still beats Lou Bega's entry:
    2.4.1 One-hit wonder status
    2.4.2 Conversion to assistant manager at greater Tampa Bay area Claim Jumper restaurant

The Happening (2008 film)

Victoria Clark as Nursery Owner's Wife, the wife of the nursery owner.

The critics can go to hell. With twists like this, we say Shyamalan has never been more unpredictable!

http://en.wikipedia.org/wiki/The_Happening_(2008_film)

Embrace of the Vampire

Many people criticized the movie as an excuse for Milano to shed her "good girl" image. Others rushed to see the movie because of that.[citation needed]

A third group spent time they should have been using to write a book about bad Wikipedia writing scouring image searches to determine just exactly how much of her "good girl" image Milano shed in this movie.

Espionage

Corporate spies nearby are a good thing as long if they do not do anything illegal; it means that your product is valuable[citation needed]

Corporate spies who do not do anything illegal are often referred to as "employees," and most successful businesses will have at least a few of them on the payroll.

http://en.wikipedia.org/wiki/Espionage

Werewolf

In Mexico, there is a belief in a creature called the nahual, which traditionally limits itself to stealing cheese and raping women rather than murder.

Remember, Mexican men, if you receive a tearful call from your wife who informs you that the Nahual has been in the house, "Dear god is the cheese ok!?" is always the wrong first response.

http://en.wikipedia.org/wiki/Werewolf

List of Kim Possible characters

For the sake of Rufus as a character, the show ignores the reality of literal naked mole rats, who are nearly completely blind, rely upon large colony environments and specific temperatures, and cannot survive individually as pets. This has led to the disappointment of many fans who have sought a pet naked mole rat and have found that not only are they unable to be pets, but look and act very little like Rufus in real life.

> *If you find yourself disappointed upon learning that real life naked mole rats do not share traits with Rufus such as eating Mexican food, a dislike of monkeys, and mastering Yamanouchi ninja techniques, experts recommend eating an entire jar of paste and then turning three years old.*

Weinerville

Since its premiere, Weinerville has drawn the attention of such shows as Entertainment Tonight, Good Morning America and The Early Show for being television's first and only half-man/half-puppet variety show where kids are transformed into puppet citizens.

The tearful parents appeared on these programs to beg the cruel producers of Weinerville to transform their beloved children back into flesh and blood. The producers merely cackled and ordered their army of puppet citizens to look their former parents in the eyes with a blank expression and tell them that their real home was Weinerville now and that they never loved them.

Silver lining? All the shows in pre-production that were planning on ripping off the "half-man/ half-puppet variety show where kids are transformed into puppet citizens" format scrapped their plans after the hailstorm of negative publicity, cementing Weinerville's status as the first and only show of its kind.

http://en.wikipedia.org/wiki/Weinerville

Hatari!

There is much fan debate about the scene where Red Buttons' character Pockets steps on the cheetah's (named Sonya) tail. On the one hand, the reactions of the cast are so natural that they seem scripted. On the other, Sonya's reaction is so genuine that it seems completely real. The debate continues.

No, it really doesn't.

http://en.wikipedia.org/wiki/Hatari!

Elisha Cuthbert

Personal life

In 2005, she maintained a blog on the National Hockey League website, though she did not post for most of the season.

> *NHL Headquarters, Manhattan:*
> *"Sir, these printouts can't be right. Elisha Cuthbert hasn't updated her blog in three months, but it's still being refreshed once every six seconds."*
>
> *"Elisha Cuthbert's blog? That was just something her agent reluctantly agreed to have her personal assistant ghostwrite! Let me see that... Dear god, these are all coming from one IP address!"*
>
> *"Yes sir. We looked it up. He's been editing her Wikipedia page too. He's shirtless in a linoleum floored basement and appears fully prepared to start jacking it as soon as she posts an entry."*
>
> *"Wow... Do IP addresses really... They tell you that much huh? Hm... You know what, I'm gonna go install a proxy, I'll be right back. And dammit, whatever you do, don't let Cuthbert's agent's personal assistant post anything on that blog!"*

http://en.wikipedia.org/wiki/Elisha_Cuthbert

Babar the Elephant

Despite the presence of these counsellors, Babar's rule seems to be totally independent of any elected body, and completely autocratic; however his leadership style seems to be one that works for the overall benefit of his elephant subjects; a form of benevolent dictator.

This one actually had a citation! It was a grainy video, apparently shot in a cave. A confused looking Cornelius the Elephant blinks rapidly, attempting to adjust his eyes to his dimly lit surroundings. He sports several days of stubble and can be heard asking for water. Frequently looking over at someone standing off-camera, he robotically asserts that Babar is a benevolent dictator, that he was wrong to have called for democratic elections, and that his claims of a government forced sterilization program were all a lie. At one point, Zephir the Monkey enters the frame. As he rears back to slap him, the video feed cuts out and when it resumes, Cornelius appears to be missing a tusk.

From the embassy of a neighboring country, Cornelius's family issued a statement that they hold out hope his body will turn up someday.

http://en.wikipedia.org/wiki/Babar_the_Elephant

National Union Attack

A scandal was caused in 2006 by Attack's observer at the European Parliament Dimitar Stoyanov (who is also Volen Siderov's stepson). Stoyanov sent an email to all MEPs that appeared to belittle Roma women. The email said of Hungarian politician Lívia Járóka, "In my country there are tens of thousands of Gypsy girls way more pretty than this honorable one… you may even buy one, around 12-13 years, to be your loving wife."

Apologists later claimed the e-mail was not intended to spark a public relations nightmare.

It was intended to spark a violent race war! Doesn't anyone in Eastern Europe know how to do a violent race war these days?

http://en.wikipedia.org/wiki/National_Union_Attack

C. Everett Koop

Even though we're told Dr. Koop remarried in 2010, after the death of his first wife, he says in a commercial for Life alert products: "With Life Alert you can live alone without being alone. That's why I wear one." So, unless the commercial is a carry-over from before 2010, he apparently doesn't live with his wife.

It's also possible that Koop meant that he lived emotionally alone, which makes sense, as that beard is basically a sign that says "I DON'T KNOW HOW TO TALK TO A WOMAN" in big, bold letters.

http://en.wikipedia.org/wiki/C._Everett_Koop

Exclusive or

Similarly, a lunch special consisting of one meat, french fries or mashed potatoes and vegetable would consist of three items, only one of which would be a form of potato. If one wanted to have meat and both kinds of potatoes, one would ask if it were possible to substitute a second order of potatoes for the vegetable. And, one would not expect to be permitted to have both types of potato and vegetable, because the result would be a vegetable plate rather than a meat plate.

Educators thought that combining school cafeteria lunches with lessons in formal logic would provide a fun way to learn, but were unprepared for the emotionally scarred students this program would produce.

https://en.wikipedia.org/wiki/Exclusive_or

Monarchy of the Netherlands

The King may cease being King in any of four ways:

Death
A dead person cannot be King.

There are a number of good practical reasons for this rule, many of which were explored in the hit 1988 film Weekend at King Willem IV's: Hijinks at the Hague.

https://en.wikipedia.org/wiki/Monarchy_of_the_Netherlands

Generic citrus sodas

Mountain Holler is a generic brand soft drink similar to Mountain Dew and is sold exclusively at Save-A-Lot grocery stores. It is also touted as a "radical citrus thirst blaster" and has a small, but cult-like group following around the U.S.[citation needed]

> You probably got a chuckle imagining the "cult-like" group that enjoys Mountain Holler. Some chubby gamers swigging it or perhaps ironic college students that initially only bought it because it was cheaper, but now claim to like it better than real Mountain Dew.
>
> But no, he really meant they're like a cult. They're twisted. They carved R.C.T.B. into the chest of an infant son of a member who had attempted to escape.

Flavor Aid

The Jonestown mass suicide, which inspired the phrase to "drink the kool-aid", was actually perpetrated with Flavor Aid.

Ironically, Flavor Aid does not have a cult-like group following around the U.S.

http://en.wikipedia.org/wiki/Flavor_Aid

Donald in Mathmagic Land

Goofs

Despite this being a mathematics educational film, a character incorrectly recites the value of the mathematical constant pi. The character states, "Pi is equal to 3.141592653589**47**, et cetera, et cetera, et cetera". The correct value of pi (to the same number of digits) is actually 3.141592653589**93**.

> *Donald Duck responded to this egregious affront to mathematical accuracy by continuing to not wear any pants.*

WrestleMania XXVI

Wrestlers portrayed a villain or a hero as they followed a series of events that built tension, and culminated in a wrestling match or series of matches.

Also, grown men in their underpants hit each other with chairs.

http://en.wikipedia.org/wiki/WrestleMania_XXVI

Doggystyle

Title significance
The album's title alludes to the Doggy style sex position and is a reference to the musician's name.

Which is, of course, Calvin Cordozar Doggystyle-Broadus, Jr.

http://en.wikipedia.org/wiki/Doggystyle

Disembowelment

If a living creature is disemboweled, it is invariably fatal without medical attention.

> Go ahead and disembowel the dead ones, though. You can't hurt them. The worst you can do is cause emotional distress to their families.

http://en.wikipedia.org/wiki/Disembowelment

Henry I of Navarre

After a brief reign, characterised, it is said, by dignity and talent, he died in July 1274, suffocated, according to the generally received accounts, by his own fat.

If you ever encounter any Ren Faire types going on and on about how Ye Olden Days were so much better than our modern world, you might want to clue them in to how low the bar was set for "dignity" in the 13th century.

http://en.wikipedia.org/wiki/Henry_I_of_Navarre

Ziggy (comic strip)

In "What a Nigga Know?" by Hip Hop group KMD, Zev Love X raps, "Livin' like that Ziggy from the funnies cat (Yeah) We both be in the papers...". (This reference was not sanctioned or approved by the comic character's creator) [citation needed].

Ziggy's creator Tom Wilson took the unsanctioned reference personally and swiftly retaliated. Many consider the response cartoon, where Ziggy attempts to return a KMD album to a department store by saying "I don't buy records by blacks" a low point in the strip's history.

http://en.wikipedia.org/wiki/Ziggy_(comic_strip)

Full House

Warner Brothers, the owners of Full House, would not permit others to use their characters, and selected who could write books based on the TV series. Such strict control by the owners of Full House means they may be considered more than fan fiction, and in fact represent a parallel universe known to many fans as the Book Universe.

If you're reading a prose tale detailing the adventures of the Tanner clan, make sure that it has been authorized by the soulless media conglomerate that owns the intellectual property rights to the Full House characters. If it does, it is 100% authentic and true. If not, it is basically a pile of garbage. Choose wisely.

http://en.wikipedia.org/wiki/Full_House

Mr. Clean

Mr. Clean has always smiled, except for a brief time in the mid-1960s during the "Mean Mr. Clean" series of ads when he was frowning because he hated dirt.

The campaign was criticized, partly because children found the mean version of the once-beloved mascot intimidating, but mostly because of the unnecessarily dark and complex backstory that Proctor & Gamble came up with to explain Mr. Clean's new attitude. In it, Dirt forced Mr. Clean to renounce cleanliness on his wedding day by kidnapping and threatening to kill his bride-to-be. A principled man of integrity, Mr. Clean of course refused, so Dirt showed him a remote feed of the bridal party tied up in a van and killed one of them at random. Mr. Clean finally broke and renounced cleanliness and promised to serve Dirt, but Dirt just laughed and killed the rest of the bridal party and Clean's fiancé anyway, then folded its arms in a hollow mockery of of the broken man's trademark gesture as it flew away in a helicopter.

Yeah, lots of people opted to just buy Scrubbing Bubbles instead while all that that was going on. Since they're pretty much the same thing and all.

http://en.wikipedia.org/wiki/Mr._Clean

The Year of the Angry Rabbit

Much more than just a sci-fi novel about giant rabbits, it is a savagely humorous indictment of war, nationalism and capitalism.

But don't worry, if giant, angry rabbits are what arouses you, you can still masturbate to it and everything.

http://en.wikipedia.org/wiki/The_Year_of_the_Angry_Rabbit

Clinical death

When the heartbeat stops, a person is suffering clinical death - by definition, but consciousness is not lost until 15-20 seconds later. Up to this point, a person doesn't feel anything about the critical situation[citation needed].

> "Huh, my heart stopped beating! Well, I'm still conscious and all, so I'm sure this will all work out fine."

http://en.wikipedia.org/wiki/Clinical_death

Flirting

Footsie, a form of flirtation in which people use their feet to play with each others' feet. This generally takes place under a table or in bed while rubbing feet. Participants often remove their shoes and play barefoot; however, it can also be played in socks, or wearing shoes. Though this method can backfire, as the general opinion of feet can depend on the culture and society of the area.

> *It can also depend on the grossness of your feet. Are your feet gross? Assess this carefully before initiating a game of footsie. The stakes are very high.*

http://en.wikipedia.org/wiki/Flirting

Ditech

On September 11, 2001 during a break on CNN in the United States, a Ditech commercial was running before being cut midway, to announce that a plane had struck one of the Twin Towers of the World Trade Center. This would then begin CNN's ongoing live footage of the September 11 attacks.

Most scientists now believe that the past decade of war and terrorism has actually been an elaborate and immersive Ditech ad. It is estimated that we will get to the part where we learn why all this death and carnage means we should refinance our mortgage with Ditech by 2018 at the latest.

http://en.wikipedia.org/wiki/Ditech

Penis enlargement

Jelqing is generally considered the safest method of penis enlargement, with the most common side effect being the dreaded "turkey necking" of the penis, which is harmless but often considered cosmetically undesirable[citation needed].

Really? [Citation Needed]? We don't even know what the hell "turkey necking" means, but if we've come to the point as a society where the claim "A turkey-necked penis is cosmetically undesirable" cannot be accepted as an outright fact, we're not sure how humanity moves on from here.

Channing Tatum

Tatum suffered a burn injury from an accident while filming The Eagle in Scotland. A crew member poured boiling water down Tatum's wetsuit, having forgotten to dilute the boiling water with cold river water, a technique used to keep actors warm during the shooting of a river-scene. Tatum attempted to pull the wetsuit away from his body, but the water poured down into the crotch of his wetsuit and severely burned his penis. Tatum reported the boiling water "pretty much burned the skin off the head of my dick" and that "it was the most painful thing I have ever experienced in my life." However, Tatum reports that "Now my penis is fantastic! One hundred percent recovered."

"My turkey neck has never looked better!"

http://en.wikipedia.org/wiki/Channing_Tatum

SMS language

The reader must interpret the abbreviated words depending on the context in which it is used, as there are many examples of words or phrases that use the same abbreviations (e.g., lol could mean laugh out loud or lots of love, and cryncould mean crayon or cryin(g)). So if someone says ttyl, lol they probably meantalk to you later, lots of love not talk to you later, laugh out loud, and if someone says omg, lol they probably mean oh my god, laugh out loud not oh my god, lots of love. "onw" means "oh no way!" nothing else.

> It could theoretically mean "otters now weaned," but of course otters' webbed paws make texting impossible for them.

http://en.wikipedia.org/wiki/SMS_language

Salad dressing spread

Salad dressing spread claims to taste like mayonnaise or to be different from mayonnaise depending on who is marketing it. Both have their supporters.

These supporters would no doubt viciously brawl to the death if not for the extreme sluggishness brought on by their terribly blocked arteries.

http://en.wikipedia.org/wiki/Salad_dressing_spread

List of James Bond henchmen in Diamonds Are Forever

It is strongly implied (though not confirmed) in the film that the two are lovers. They are seen holding hands in one scene; and at one point, Mr. Kidd remarks that Tiffany Case is attractive, only to receive a glare from Mr. Wint, prompting him to add, "…for a lady". Mr. Wint can also be seen spraying himself with perfume, although this clearly isn't a sign of homosexuality.

> *The fact that Mr. Kidd was blowing him while he was spraying himself with perfume is a tad less ambiguous.*

Disneymania

Britney Spears was originally also going to be on the album, with the song "It's a Small World", also appearing on the original cover, but it's not sure what happened.

We were going to speculate that maybe Britney Spears had too much dignity to record a song so closely associated with hundreds of tiny shrieking robotic ethnic stereotypes, but then we realized, ha ha, Britney Spears, dignity, that can't be right.

http://en.wikipedia.org/wiki/Disneymania

Rabbit rabbit rabbit

Traditions also extend to saying on the first of each month: "A pinch and a punch for the first day of the month; white rabbit!" White rabbit is declared to be the "no returns" policy on the "pinch and the punch" the receiver felt. A small concession exists, for recipients of the "pinch and a punch", where white rabbit declaration (no returns) is not made. Recipients may in this case reply with "A flick and a kick for being so quick." In some areas, it is simply, "Pinch, punch, first the month, no returns back!" Additionally, there is a way to defeat the white rabbit/no returns declaration. This is by introducing magic mirror glue. The following is an example of such a play, Person 1: "Hey X, a pinch and a punch for the first day of the month; white rabbit!" Person 2: "Not happening Y, I declare Magic Mirror Glue, today's punches and kicks bounce off me and stick to you!" Person 2 is then free to pinch/punch/kick said instigator.

Excepting of course, instances of Jinx being called during simultaneous claims, for which we refer you to Section 10.3-7b of the Uniform Bullshit Code.

http://en.wikipedia.org/wiki/Rabbit_rabbit_rabbit

Three Billy Goats Gruff

The story introduces three male goats, sometimes identified in the story as youngster, father and grandfather, but more often described as brothers. It appears to be a masculinity myth, but not necessarily so.

The only possible way you'd have mistook this story for a masculinity myth is if you'd flushed years of your life down the drain attaining the type of bullshit advanced degree that discusses things like "masculinity myths." The author of this entry, who clearly has done exactly this, believes that your degree is worthless, as clearly the Three Billy Goats Gruff does not fall into this category, and furthermore do you please have any leads on eighth grade substitute teaching gigs? Mom's going to start making me pay rent really soon.

http://en.wikipedia.org/wiki/Three_Billy_Goats_Gruff

Oxyrhynchus

The town was named after a species of fish of the Nile River which was important in Egyptian mythology as the fish that ate the penis of Osiris, though it is not known exactly which species of fish this is.

One: Screw the construction of the pyramids and the invention of paper. Managing to name a town after a fish whose name is unknown ranks as the Egyptian's top achievement as a society.

Two: How is it not the top priority of any male on the face of the Earth who has ever set foot in water to find out exactly which species of fish this is?

https://en.wikipedia.org/wiki/Oxyrhynchus

A Visit From St. Nicholas

In A Muppet Family Christmas, the Sesame Street Muppets perform a play based on the poem, with Ernie narrating as the father (the main character) and Bert as Mamma (he lost a coin toss). The monsters appear as the reindeer, with the Two-Headed Monster as Santa (and Grover as the mouse who is not stirring, literally). The narration omits the line "The children were nestled, all snug in their bed(s)/While visions of sugar plums danced in their heads", because of the homosexuality rumor.[citation needed]

> The Muppets are now censoring themselves because of longstanding rumors about Tom Cruise being gay? Seems arbitrary and weird, but who are we to judge?

Yavin

All except three Rebel Alliance craft were destroyed in the attack, the only survivors being Luke Skywalker, Wedge Antilles, and an unnamed Y-wing pilot (perhaps Keyan Farlander), and possibly a gunner, making four, not including Luke.

Fans began to wonder if Disney's new Star Wars movie was anything more than just a rushed cash grab when this troubling excerpt from the opening scrolling text of Episode 7 leaked to the internet.

Cultural depictions of Joan of Arc

1968 - The Image of the Beast Philip José Farmer Joan of Arc is portrayed as an alien sexual predator, still alive in the 20th century but with her body altered to enable the also-alien 15th-century serial killer Gilles de Rais to live within her vagina dentata as a fang-toothed venomous snake that bites and paralyses men during intercourse.

Also, in Bill & Ted she taught aerobics at the mall.

http://en.wikipedia.org/wiki/Cultural_depictions_of_Joan_of_Arc

Jolly Rancher

Fruit punch is based on fruit.

> *This comes as a major surprise to everyone who assumed it was based on the novel* Push *by Sapphire.*

http://en.wikipedia.org/wiki/Jolly_Rancher

alt.sex.stories

The newsgroup quickly became one of the most popular text-based newsgroups (i.e. not intended for posting binary files) on Usenet. Amateur writers of all sorts began posting fictional "erotic stories" and finding a worldwide audience for their work. However, because of the very nature of unmoderated newsgroups, alt.sex.stories soon found itself a repository for a great number of poorly-written, sometimes barely coherent "stroke" stories consisting of a few sentences or paragraphs. The average quality of the stories posted to the newsgroup seemed somewhat lower and more crude than the stories seen in pornographic magazines and books, and this state of affairs continues to the current day.[citation needed]

> Yes, the "stroke" stories certainly undermined the credibility of the newsgroup that had produced stories such as "Balling Lil' Sis," "Showtime - Part 6 Featuring Jennifer Love Hewitt and a Vanna White Lookalike," and "Alex and Brian," which features the immortal sentence "'Shhhhhhh, if you do as i say you wont get this!' he said as he pulled out a 12 inch dildo with the name 'MegaMan' on it."

http://en.wikipedia.org/wiki/Alt.sex.stories

Nick Kroll

Kroll is one of the co-authors of the critically acclaimed book Bar Mitzvah Disco and a graduate of Rye Country Day School, where he gave a contentious graduation speech in which, contrary to widespread belief, he did not expose his genitals, although he did gently chastise the school administration.

This came as a relief to Rye Country Day School valedictorian Kyle Verlan, who was speaking after Kroll and had pretty much based his entire commencement speech around whipping it out.

http://en.wikipedia.org/wiki/Nick_Kroll

Juliette (novel)

A long audience with Pope Pius VI is one of the most extensive scenes in Juliette. The heroine shows off her learning to the Pope (whom she most often addresses by his secular name "Braschi") with a verbal catalogue of alleged immoralities committed by his predecessors. The audience ends, like almost every other scene in the narrative, with an orgy.

The Vatican used to send up black smoke to indicate that an orgy was imminent, giving cardinals time to make their way to St. Peter's Basilica (aka the Bone Dome). Nowadays, the meaning is of course quite different: black smoke indicates that a Papal conclave was unable to elect a new pope. Usually this is because instead of voting, they just ended up having an orgy.

http://en.wikipedia.org/wiki/Juliette_(novel)

Latin for All Occasions

The translations are mostly direct, so an English expression like "Get your ducks in a row" is translated as *Anates tuas in acie instrue*. The significance of having ducks lined up would presumably be a mystery to an ancient Roman, or indeed to a non-American.

British Wikipedians: There is literally no article where you can't somehow wedge in "how dare Americans think their idioms are understood by all English speakers" outrage, if you really work at it.

http://en.wikipedia.org/wiki/Latin_for_All_Occasions

List of gestures

Blow job gesture is made by curling the fingers into a loose fist and moving the hand back and forth in front of the mouth, while the lips is making rounded "o" shape, as though performing fellatio. The gesture usually enchanced with the tongue pricking the inner wall of the cheek. The gesture is considered as a lewd or obscene gesture and depends to the context, may implying some different things linked to fellatio, such as; to inform somebody that someone is performing actual oral sex, offering one, asking one, as a taunting gesture to insult someone as male homosexual or as insulting gesture which means someone is doing sucking up.[better source needed]

> *For the love of god people, get some citations in there! This passage about the blow job gesture is almost entirely devoid of intellectual honesty!*

http://en.wikipedia.org/wiki/List_of_gestures

Church of Our Lady before Týn

Highlights

-The northern portal is a wonderful example of Gothic sculpture from the Parler workshop, with a relief depicting the Crucifixion. The main entrance is located on the church's western face, through a narrow passage between the houses in front of the church.

-The early baroque altarpiece has paintings by Karel Škréta from around 1649.

-The oldest pipe organ in Prague stands inside this church. The organ was built in 1673 by Heinrich Mundt and is one of the most representative 17th-century organs in Europe.

-The great Danish astronomer Tycho Brahe, who worked for Emperor Rudolph II, was buried in the church in 1601. His beautiful marble tomb slab is located inside.

-The church appears in the start of the Revolution Films movie xXx

Just another example of the United States' obscure but longstanding policy: bury an influential scientist in an architecturally important landmark, and if it's still standing after two World Wars, we'll grease up Vin Diesel and send him over there.

http://en.wikipedia.org/wiki/Church_of_Our_Lady_before_T%C3%BDn

List of brassiere designs

Novelty

A fashion bra designed for appearance and sensuality. May include unusual materials, like leather or feathers. Includes unusual designs like the open-tip, peekaboo, or peephole bra that feature holes or slits in the fabric that reveal the woman's areola and nipples. Usually made of sensuous material like Lycra, nylon (nylon tricot), polyester, satin, lace and/or silk. Suitable for erotic situations.

> *If you ever see an item tagged "suitable for erotic situations" in a Home Depot, flee the premises immediately.*

http://en.wikipedia.org/wiki/List_of_brassiere_designs

Moondragon

Moondragon's most notable characteristics are her shaved head, superiority complex, and gruelling elite excellence in virtually every area a human being can achieve.

It must suck to go through the presumably arduous effort of achieving gruelling elite excellence in virtually every area a human being can achieve and then still have people lead with "bald chick" when introducing you.

http://en.wikipedia.org/wiki/Moondragon

Fenimore Cooper's Literary Offenses

Mark Twain is a notoriously harsh critic of his contemporaries. His style of critical analysis is humorous, but altogether not too different from any sort of stand-up comedy burns we see today.

None other than Ernest Hemingway declared that "All modern American literature comes from Twain's classic burn about how steamboat captains travelling northbound on the Mississippi be hailing wood-lot foremen for information on river depth like this, but steamboat captains travelling southbound on the Mississippi be hailing wood-lot foremen for information on river depth like this!"

http://en.wikipedia.org/wiki/Fenimore_Cooper%27s_Literary_Offenses

Stinkers Bad Movie Awards

The Stinkers initially opened their balloting to the general moviegoing public but soon discovered that most people surveyed hadn't seen many of the films on the ballot and often just voted for the person they hated the most, usually someone like Mariah Carey, the Spice Girls or anyone connected with the film Gigli.

Academy Award voters admitted that this was the same method they employed in selecting "Argo" as best picture.

http://en.wikipedia.org/wiki/Stinkers_Bad_Movie_Awards

Battle Cat

He has the appearance of a green, orange-striped tiger. In the episode "Teela's Quest", Queen Marlena says to Adam in regards to the planet Earth, "There are no talking green tigers on Earth." It is not known if her referring to Cringer as a tiger means he is called a tiger on Eternia, or if she is simply using it as a comparison, but in the episode "A Beastly Sideshow" Evil-Lyn also refers to Cringer as a tiger, and in the episode "House of Shokoti", a boy is surprised that he is "a talking tiger", so presumably, Cringer would be seen as a tiger on Eternia. However, his species is never given an explicit name and it is unclear how many others like him there are.

Next on this author's to-do list? His 35,000-word dissertation "Indications and Circumstantial Evidence That Stinkor: The Evil Master of Odors May Have Been Modeled After a Skunk."

http://en.wikipedia.org/wiki/Battle_Cat

List of Star Wars species (U–Z)

Yuzzum
They have been exported as pets, but are not very good at it.

As a society that considers a Betta fish in a five ounce plastic cup of water a legitimate pet, let us take a moment to consider what would make a Yuzzum bad at being a pet. Explosive feces, right? It has to be explosive feces.

Everything's Ducky

Plot

Two sailors sneak a talking duck aboard their ship. Complications ensue. The duck waddles all over the ship until he escapes.

> Sadly, the "complications" that "ensued" left dozens of children fatherless.

http://en.wikipedia.org/wiki/Everything's_Ducky

Noah Ringer

Character

Many people admire Noah, not just to do a good job as an actor but also a great person, Noah loves his fans, he is always wanting a good weekend for everyone on Facebook. Sometimes, Noah asks for prayers to help someone or some cause. Fans of Noah return the love, always sending positive messages to him. Your Brazilian fans in particular show a certain kind of love, his Brazilian fans really loves him.

Noah Ringer was found dead in a Brazilian guy's basement three months later. His nipples had been cut off.

http://en.wikipedia.org/wiki/Noah_Ringer

Serendipity (book series)

The animals in the Serendipity books include both real animals such as bears,cats, dogs, horses, squirrels, rabbits. There also are mythical creatures, such as unicorns, dragons, sea monsters, and pegasus to name a few. Cosgrove also invented his own creatures such as the wheedle, hucklebug and kritter.

The stories told in the series teach children important lessons because they are based on real-life situations.

Real-life situations, such as "What to do if you hit a Wheedle with your station wagon," "How to politely refuse Kritter if served it at a dinner party," and "Overcoming grief if a Hucklebug bores into your grandmother's liver and lays eggs that mature and hatch faster than anyone could have predicted, eventually gnawing their way out while she's yelling at you to change channels with 'the clicker.'"

Freddy Moore

Moore soon became the San Fernando Valley's answer to England's Jeff Lynne, the guiding influence behind the Electric Light Orchestra. Although ELO's orchestrated pop style bears absolutely no resemblance to the rocky bebop sound of Moore's group, The Kats, the two bands have one thing in common – strong leadership.

Also, they both produced noises that could be described as "music," and all members of both bands were bipedal primates.

http://en.wikipedia.org/wiki/Freddy_Moore

Fellatio

Importantly, the testes are also a male erogenous zone.

Honey? Remember that argument we had last night? About you know what-ing my you know whats? Well, I think that if you'll just check Wikipedia you'll see that it's in agreement with me about the importance of that particular act. Honey, what are you doing? I think this issue has been-whoa! Whoa! No need to check that edit history! I'm sure that claim has been on there for years! Well, sure but anybody could have made that edit last night five minutes after you went to bed. Honey? Honey? I know you're not asleep. Honey?

https://en.wikipedia.org/wiki/Fellatio

Shiatsu

Shiatsu is usually performed on a futon mat, with clients fully clothed. It is also performed on horses.[citation needed]

Wait, are the horses fully clothed or not? Asking for a friend who moderates an active NSFW Deviantart horse massage art community.

If Day

If Day included a staged firefight between Canadian troops and volunteers dressed as Nazi soldiers, the internment of prominent politicians, the imposition of Nazi rule, and a parade.

You may disagree with their policies on world conquest, ethnic purity, and genocide, but darn it, those guys knew how to do a parade, am I right?

http://en.wikipedia.org/wiki/If_Day

Human gastrointestinal tract

The lower gastrointestinal tract includes most of the small intestine and all of the large intestine. According to some sources, it also includes the anus.[citation needed]

However, these sources must be taken with a grain of salt, as the majority of them are biased, pro-anus inclusion propaganda. These include Anus Fancy, the quarterly journal of AnusPAC, and Highlights For Children (you have to read between the lines a bit on that last one, but trust us, it's there).

http://en.wikipedia.org/wiki/Human_gastrointestinal_tract

Last words

Last words may be deliberately misquoted in official records, or family members may enhance or create last words in order to further the reputation of the deceased. For example, Vice-Admiral Horatio Nelson's last words were probably "Drink, drink. Fan, fan. Rub, rub",[citation needed] but he is remembered for his earlier words "Kiss me Hardy", when mortally wounded; George V's last words were reputedly "Bugger Bognor", but official records reported that he was inquiring about the British Empire.[citation needed]

> George V was the last British monarch to take seriously the ancient royal duty of sodomizing entire towns at every opportunity.

Sexy son hypothesis

In particular, it has been shown that human females are more attracted to men of higher physical attractiveness.

*This study also put forth the controversial theory that ice is cold and fire is hot. But never fear, hideous men! The same study showed that **bovine** females are DTF men of lower physical attractiveness anytime, anywhere.*

Bidet

The electronics in many attachable bidets draws the attention of those who like gadgets. Gadgets capture the imagination. They allow us to do things that we never thought possible. With a bidet remote control, the gadget factor goes through the roof. You can have things happen without touching anything on the attachment itself. That is a real attraction for many. They learn to like the benefits while gaining entertainment from the remote control features. This trend will continue as manufacturers add more features to bidet seats and more buttons to the remote. This is one of the better trends out there.

RELEVANT WORK EXPERIENCE

Social media marketing strategist, North American Bidet Council, June 2011–Present

*Helped raise awareness of under-promoted advances in bidet technology to potential new interest groups across a number of online social platforms

http://en.wikipedia.org/wiki/Bidet

Juicy (The Notorious B.I.G. song)

The song is a "rags-to-riches chronicle" detailing his early years in poverty, his initial dreams of becoming a rap artist and early influences, his time in drugs and crime, and his eventual success in the music business and ownership of both a Super Nintendo and a Sega Genesis.

While Biggie's violent death was a tragedy for music fans everywhere, we can take solace in knowing that during his all-too-brief lifetime he was at least able to achieve his lifelong dream of owning multiple 16-bit video game consoles.

http://en.wikipedia.org/wiki/Juicy_(The_Notorious_B.I.G._song)

Hamster ball

Children should not throw, drop, or bounce hamster balls.[citation needed]

This [citation needed] was added by the Underground Gerbil Liberation armY (U.G.L.Y.) as part of their decades-long war against the hamsters. They hope that by subtly vandalizing various Wikipedia articles, they can encourage humans to harm hamsters, assisting the gerbils in their efforts to wipe them out.

Yes, it's an idiotic, terrible plan. What the hell do you expect? They're gerbils!

http://en.wikipedia.org/wiki/Hamster_ball

There Was an Old Lady Who Swallowed a Fly

The joke of the song comes from the fact that the woman clearly should have died after swallowing the bird, but manages to swallow even more animals of ridiculous sizes with no problem and survives, and yet she suddenly dies after swallowing a horse (which is not much larger than the donkey she swallows and possibly even smaller than the cow she swallowed earlier).

Yes, that part's the joke. The rest of the song is deadly serious.

http://en.wikipedia.org/wiki/There_Was_an_Old_Lady_Who_Swallowed_a_Fly

Car numberplate game

If you call out a license plate that has already been named, or you yell out the wrong state, you have to punch yourself in the face or pull out a hair from your head as a penalty. This is also possible in Ireland.

It's possible to punch yourself in the face anywhere, but it's more socially acceptable in Ireland. Downright encouraged, really. Go on then, just wind up and give yourself a good bash right in the kisser! You'll feel better after! I mean, you won't, but still.

http://en.wikipedia.org/wiki/Car_numberplate_game

Fear of a Black Hat

Tone Def (Mark Christopher Lawrence), the esoteric D.J., who is talented enough to scratch with his butt and his penis (the latter is not shown directly, but strongly and humorously implied).

*Humorously? No, dammit, you completely misinterpreted the "implied penis scratching" scene! It was supposed to be filled with ennui and self-loathing! How could your interpretation have been so far off? Was our implication not strong enough? Or perhaps **too strong**? Was it a mistake to replace the traditional DJ scratching onomatopoeia "Wikki Wikki" with "Dicky Dicky" while Tone Def was scratching with his penis? Or maybe the scene where one of the hoes in the club asked the DJ if he would spin the new seven inch and the record scratches while he raises his eyebrows at the camera?*

Well at the very least you didn't think that the butt scratching scene was supposed to be funny, did you? Oh come on!!

http://en.wikipedia.org/wiki/Fear_of_a_Black_Hat

Herbal cigarette

Plus they have a lack of any other physically addictive substance in them, because of this, they are not physically addictive.

The lack of health risks from physical addiction are unfortunately more than balanced out by the severe health risk of getting repeatedly punched in the face by strangers for being the kind of douche that smokes herbal cigarettes.

http://en.wikipedia.org/wiki/Herbal_cigarette

Anal vibrator

An anal vibrator is a sex toy meant for sexual stimulation of the anus. Basically, all anal vibrators have one common feature - they produce a vibrating effect in the rectum for pleasurable sensations.

Is there a board ensuring that these devices meet this industry standard?

"Dear Sir, We regret to inform you that the Jar-Jar Binks action figure you submitted did not produce a vibrating effect for pleasurable sensations in the rectum of our test subject. Thus, it cannot be certified as a board-approved anal vibrator. We will be testing the rest of the box of potential devices you sent us as soon as our subject has recovered. Sincerely, The Anal Vibrator Certification Board (AVCB)."

Keep Portland Weird

The slogan has inspired a variety of articles that attempt to quantify whether or not Portland is "weird". The consensus is that Portland is one of the weirder major cities in the U.S.[citation needed]

Anxious, self-absorbed attempts to come to consensus on some quantification of weirdness? This slogan just gets more and more Portland as you peel back the layers.

http://en.wikipedia.org/wiki/Keep_Portland_Weird

Balneario

It is a specific recreational destination with features such as bathrooms, lifeguards, changing rooms, snack stands, banana boats, kayak rentals, surfboard rental, lifejacket rental, water toy rental, wetsuit rental, sporting good rental, scuba diving, swimming and surfing lessons, parasailing, picnic tables, lounge chairs and umbrellas, gift and souvenir shops, prostitutes and strippers, parades, circuses, concerts, rallies, contests, live music, street performers, live entertainment, bonfires, fresh seafood, smoothies, barbecue, camping, gambling, alcohol, and street food vendors.

Some unscrupulous proprietors have the nerve to label their recreational destination a Balneario despite not offering lifejacket rental or prostitutes. Both are as essential to the Balneario experience as rallies and banana boats. Do your part to prevent Balneario fraud and leave these con artists viciously negative feedback on tripadvisor.com.

http://en.wikipedia.org/wiki/Balneario

Empty nest syndrome

In order to fill the void of the empty house, many people look for something that is living and breathing that will take their mind off of their feelings, like a pet.

"A pet?" the husband said. "No, no, of course I understood that's what you were getting at honey." He nervously glanced over his shoulder at the large, writhing gunny sack that sat just outside the door, wondering if the wino inside had been sober enough to identify him.

http://en.wikipedia.org/wiki/Empty_nest_syndrome

Werther's Original

One UK advert consisted of a montage of the grandfather and grandson bonding together (for example, pointing at animals out of train windows).

The ad was considered far too edgy by Werther's target audience, who complained that the train moved too fast and the animals had no business being that colorful. Furthermore, they asserted that the grandson pointed too much and did not seem nearly reluctant enough to take the weird candy that his grandfather was always offering him. Werther's relented and reshot the ad to include a scene of the grandson calling his friends in amazement to tell them that his grandfather still used something called "WebTV."

http://en.wikipedia.org/wiki/Werther's_Original

Sega Bass Fishing

Gameplay

Bass Fishing is an arcade fishing game. Basically, someone choses a character then goes out on a boat to go and catch fish.

Unlockable mini-games where you ignore texts from your wife and wait for your buddy to propose another round of beers because you think that him suggesting it makes you seem like less of an alcoholic are available as downloadable content.

http://en.wikipedia.org/wiki/Sega_Bass_Fishing

Cat massage

Cat massage has increased more and more in popularity given that there are cat massage therapists who are able to massage a cat by using the best techniques. Given that these therapists are actually trained and know what they are doing, it is obvious that cat massaging is important to the pet and also to the pet's owner.

You will notice that the Wikipedia page for neurosurgery does not feel the need to inform you that neurosurgeons "are actually trained and know what they are doing."

Parking

Parking is the act of stopping a vehicle and leaving it unoccupied.

> *The act is famously depicted in the popular '80s standup bit, "Why do we drive on a parkway but stop a vehicle and leave it unoccupied on a driveway?"*

Fat Freddy's Cat

The Cat is much smarter than Freddy, and is a sort of hippie Garfield (whom he predates). He tends to regard the Freak Brothers with amused contempt, frequently expressed by defecating in inappropriate and inconvenient places, such as stereo headphones.

Following the cat's lead, Insane Clown Posse have opted to forego actually recording their next album, and instead just defecate directly into Juggalos' headphones.

http://en.wikipedia.org/wiki/Fat_Freddy's_Cat

Tocco Caudio

Fortunately the local and provincial administration from the year 2000 have managed to receive government grants to rebuild the old church, mainly to resemble a sort of historical landmark, as if to erect and let emerge a flame over an empty graveyard, as sort of lighthouse, to evoke not danger, but a light of hope and goodwill to renew and start new era for all.

As the citizens of Tocco Caudio found, the best way to get grant money out of the Italian government is to present your goals in evocative, allegorical language. In possibly related news, Italy is pretty much bankrupt these days.

http://en.wikipedia.org/wiki/Tocco_Caudio

Scottish Gaelic

Where an l, n or r is followed (or in the case of m, preceded) by a b, bh, ch, g, gh, m or mh, an epenthetic vowel is inserted between the two. This is usually a copy of the vowel that preceded the l/n/r. Examples; Alba /aɫapə/, marbh /marav/, tilg /tʰʲilikʲ/, arm /aram/, iomradh/ imirəɣ/.

The sequences ms and mch are also epentheticised, just for fun.

> Hey, everyone, guess which language has been spoken in Scotland for centuries and yet is only understood by 1.2% of Scottish people today! Go on, guess!

http://en.wikipedia.org/wiki/Scottish_Gaelic

Darth Maul

Darth Maul appears in a Brisk commercial, fighting Yoda to support The Phantom Menace in 3D. He claims to have been at a wild party the night before, which causes his lightsaber to malfunction. He crashes into a Brisk vending machine, jumps up, and yells, "Double saber delicious!" before getting crushed by the vending machine.

Still a more dignified way to die than being cut in half by the star of Salmon Fishing in the Yemen.

Tundra (Comic Strip)

The main bear. Dudley is big in every imagineable way.[citation needed]

This is a tough statement to properly find a citation for, because there really are no limits to the human imagination. Also, nobody wants to measure a cartoon bear's penis.

http://en.wikipedia.org/wiki/Tundra_(comic_strip)

Action Park

Employees at the park used to like eating at a nearby snack bar with a good view of the attraction, since it was almost guaranteed that they could see some serious injuries, lost bikini tops, or both.

Seeing someone get paralyzed on a water slide was always a treat, but if a playful dog ran off with her bikini top after she'd lost the use of her lower limbs, leaving her breasts exposed until a medic or a wailing family member covered them up? It was like living out your own personal Porky's, man.

http://en.wikipedia.org/wiki/Action_Park

Jeffrey Hunter

It was said at his funeral that he was a good man.

The Hunter estate kindly requests that you ignore the fact that the speaker was simultaneously making the blow job gesture.

http://en.wikipedia.org/wiki/Jeffrey_Hunter

Woops!

The group finds a teenage delinquent has been living near the farm, and his attitude has been only worsened by the nuclear holocaust.

Crybaby.

http://en.wikipedia.org/wiki/Woops!

Garzey's Wing

The leader of the slaves, who is represented through a bearded old man, follows a strict belief that "humans are just human", which can also be understood as the moral of this tale in Byston Well. Chris is only human so he can only act as human through his human nature to protect human kind. Although it may seem to be a deep concept to grasp, the idea can easily understood after a thorough analysis of the anime.

Other ideas that may seem hard to grasp but can be easily understood after spending some time thoroughly analyzing anime: chastity, sorrow, grown men willingly wearing diapers, XXXXL sweatpants, receiving a lifetime ban from AnthroCon for attaching a large black penis to your Sonic The Hedgehog costume, and the image search results for "tentacles+hello+kitty."

The Holy Mountain (1973 film)

The Beatles member George Harrison was intended to play the main character but he withdrew when read in the script he had to wash his anus in front of the camera.

> *Ironically, just before John Lennon was murdered, Yoko Ono was encouraging him to record an experimental album that was to be just the sound of the two of them washing their anuses.*
>
> *The scary thing about their relationship is that if you had read the previous sentence somewhere with slightly more credibility than a bad Wikipedia writing book, there is a non-zero chance that you might have thought it was true.*

http://en.wikipedia.org/wiki/The_Holy_Mountain_(1973_film)

My Balls

Plot
The fate of the world rests in one man's testicles.

This is what President Obama thinks to himself when he stands naked in front of the bathroom mirror every morning.

Schroeder (Peanuts)

Relationship with Sally Brown

As his best friend's baby sister, she is originally the little annoying kid who is always tagging along. However, it was implied later on through the strips that he possibly had feelings for her. This small window for fandoms was almost completely extinguished however whenever he kissed Lucy on the cheek. Ironically, though... Sally always seemed a little more toned down and not quite as hyper and happy after that strip was published, implying that perhaps he was more than just her big brother's friend as well. However, the small possibility of Sally/Schroeder lives on in those with hope, forming the now-known Schroeder Decision in which he "chooses" Lucy over Sally.[clarification needed]

> Yeah, you know what, on second thought please do not clarify this troubling description of the romantic lives of children, and certainly do not clarify it in a 7,500-word story on fanfiction.net called "Schroeder's Decision: The Aftermath."

http://en.wikipedia.org/wiki/Schroeder_(Peanuts)

Crocodile Dentist

An episode of the The Price Is Right from 1993 featured the travel version of the game as one of the small items used in the pricing game Pathfinder. Model Janice Pennington demonstrated to host Bob Barker how the game works. After pressing a few teeth, Barker chose the bad tooth causing the crocodile to snap on Bob's hand causing Barker to incite a loud "Aaah!"

Barker actually lost two fingers above the knuckle on his right hand in the incident, but due to his obsessive professionalism, he refused to seek medical attention until the end of the day's taping. Later in the game, during the Showcase Showdown, an eagle-eyed observer would note that he kept the Big Wheel between his hand and the cameras, so as to not horrify home viewers with his bloody finger-stumps.

McDonaldland

Additional family were revealed in a McDonaldland VHS tape "The Legend of Grimace Island": Grimace has an unnamed mom, an unnamed dad, a grandma named "Winky", a great, great grandma named Jenny Grimace, and might have a brother named "King Gonga," who is the king of all Grimaces.

We're pretty sure this VHS tape was found in an abandoned, blood-stained cabin, labeled "LEGEND OF GRIMACE ISLAND" in magic marker, and seven days after you watch it a demonic Mayor McCheese crawls out of the television set and smothers you in secret sauce.

Pince-nez

In the Sonic the Hedgehog video game series, the main antagonist, Doctor Eggman wears reflective-lensed blue tinted pince-nez sunglasses to cover his eyes. What his actual eyes look like is unknown, but a lot of fans speculate they are black with red pupils, just like other counterparts.

This author has taken an article about a style of glasses popular around the turn of the 20th century and favored by President Teddy Roosevelt, and somehow managed to use it to advance their own agenda about the theoretical eye color of a video game boss. This is black-belt level bad Wikipedia writing, folks. Do not attempt to undertake such writing without the assistance of a dimwit: severe injury may be the result.

Celebration (Kool & the Gang song)

The song is also notable for having played when the remaining American hostages returned home following the 1979-1981 Iran Hostage Crisis. It was also rewritten in 1984 as the jingle for Diet Orange Crush.

> *"Look, we're happy the hostages are home, and will gladly license our tune for a slightly reduced hardship fee. But we can't go rewriting our songs for just any old event." —Kool & the Gang*

Sex Games

"Sex Games" is an adult video game developed by Landisoft in 1985. It is available just in Commodore 64.

Gameplay

The gameplay was rather simple, basically keeping a forward-backward groove.

> *"So, what should the sex in our game be like?" one virgin programmer asked another virgin programmer.*
>
> *"Oh, just like sex in real life," the second virgin said.*
>
> *"Right, of course," the first virgin replied. "But just to be sure we're on the same page, it should be..." The first virgin trailed off.*
>
> *"Well, you know..." The second virgin trailed off, stalling for time. In a panic, he glanced around the room, where a third virgin was rewinding and fast forwarding a VHS copy of the classic hip-hop film Krush Groove over and over again, going forward and backward in search of the hilarious scene where the Fat Boys shut down an all-you-can-eat restaurant.*

"Like a... forward... backward... groove?" he proposed timidly.

"Oh sure, obviously. We all know what that's like!" the first virgin replied. The third virgin smiled and nodded emphatically. All three of them stopped coding for a moment to watch the movie.

Human height

A demonstration of the height-success association can be found in the realm of politics. In the United States presidential elections, the taller candidate won 22 out of 25 times in the 20th century.[20] Nevertheless, Ignatius Loyola, founder of the Jesuits, was 1.5 m (4 ft 11 in) and several prominent world leaders of the twentieth century, such as Vladimir Lenin, Benito Mussolini, Nicolae Ceaușescu and Joseph Stalin were of below average height.

Look, we're not saying short people should be rounded up and put in camps, just that they shouldn't be allowed to vote or hold political office. That's a sensible compromise that's grounded in scientific evidence.

https://en.wikipedia.org/wiki/Human_height

York (explorer)

As William Clark's slave, he had to do difficult manual labour without pay.

> *Gee, when you put it that way, being a slave sounds kind of crappy!*

Urechis unicinctus

They are unofficially known as the "Penis Fish" due to their resemblance to male genitalia, though not necessarily human. This name is a misnomer due to the fact that they are neither penises nor fish.

When your Wikipedia page includes a variation of the phrase "Is not actually a penis," perhaps the battle to keep "penis" out of your nickname is already lost?

http://en.wikipedia.org/wiki/Urechis_unicinctus

Toadfish

Toadfish is the common name for a variety of species from several different families of fish, usually because of their toad-like appearance.

To answer the question you're no doubt asking yourself:

Yes. They are penises.

http://en.wikipedia.org/wiki/Toadfish

Imaginary friend

They may seem real to their creators, though they are ultimately unreal, as shown by studies.

"But Pappan is real!" little Billy cried. "Those studies' control groups were inadequately segregated from the program groups! And the studies were published in the Lancet! Everyone knows the Lancet is a joke!"

http://en.wikipedia.org/wiki/Imaginary_friend

Mothra

Mothra is known for her habit of dying somehow in many of the movies she has appeared in.

Essentially her catchphrase, Mothra dying was the Austin Powers saying "Yeahhhh baby!" of 1960s Toho tokusatsu films. That is to say, it was a fun breath of fresh air when the first movie kind of came out of nowhere and Mothra did her classic "dying" bit. But then in the sequels it got embarrassing really quick. Lame Japanese uncles still do their impression of Mothra dying at family gatherings, and there is a general fear among Japanese people that since her career has hit a rough patch as of late, Mothra is going to drag the bit out of the closet and make a new movie where she hits all the tired beats: dying, fighting Godzilla, holding up humorously phallic objects in front of her own, horrible moth-genitalia.

http://en.wikipedia.org/wiki/Mothra

Elizabeth Woodville

Elizabeth was called "the most beautiful woman in the Island of Britain" with "heavy-lidded eyes like those of a dragon", suggesting a perhaps unusual criterion by which beauty in late medieval England was judged.

Yes, medieval England was a technologically backwards, hyper-religious, non-democratic society by today's standards. But on the other hand, these very factors prevented the rise of an online community dedicated to hosting the dragon-themed pornography and erotic literature the population obviously craved, so who are we to say we have it better today?

http://en.wikipedia.org/wiki/Elizabeth_Woodville

House music

In the Channel 4 documentary Pump Up The Volume, Knuckles remarks that the first time he heard the term "house music" was upon seeing "we play house music" on a sign in the window of a bar on Chicago's South Side. One of the people in the car with him joked, "you know, that's the kind of music you play down at the Warehouse!", and then everybody laughed.

Was ecstasy already associated with house music at this point? Because that might explain the hysterical laughter with no obvious cause.

http://en.wikipedia.org/wiki/House_music

Real life

Real life is an actual event or life lived by real people, contrasted to that lived by fiction or fantasy characters, or real people interacting on the Internet.

Hear that, everyone? Real people interacting on the Internet doesn't count as real life! So, make your YouTube comments as racist and misspelled as you want, we guess.

http://en.wikipedia.org/wiki/Real_life

Alex Cross (film)

Cross chases Picasso and Picasso hits him with a pipe, after that Picasso and Cross fight with Picasso pinning Cross, Picasso tells him he is going to, then kicks him in his side, enjoy this, which means he is going to enjoy killing Cross, he takes out a syringe and attempts to paralyze Cross, but Cross pulls out a little pocket knife frorn Picasso's front shirt pocket and stabs him in the shoulder where his pocket is with it, this causes them to fall through the thing

Yes, it's no easy feat sneaking your laptop into the premiere of "Alex Cross" and live-updating the plot summary as the film is being shown for the very first time. But if you know of another way to make sure that Wikipedia includes the most up-to-date and accurate information on current cinema possible, we'd like to hear it.

Here Comes Honey Boo Boo

Shannon is the star of the show as much as her daughter with her extreme couponing with her family at The Piggly Wiggly, farting, sneezing, bingo playing and even her ketchup and spaghetti recipes.[clarification needed]

Yes, please clarify! Do you... put the ketchup on the spaghetti, or the spaghetti on the ketchup? Do you cook the spaghetti before adding the ketchup? How much ketchup are we talking here? One whole bottle? Two? World's most complete reference guide, my ass!

Gotō, Nagasaki

Interesting Facts

Gotō is the Cat-Battle-Capital of the world, some of the more accomplished and feral cats reside on Naru Island. However all cats in the Gotō area are in constant competition with each other.

The battle over "Who can look the most disinterested while licking their asshole for 20 minutes straight" is particularly hard fought.

http://en.wikipedia.org/wiki/Got%C5%8D,_Nagasaki

171

Western New York

Western New York consists of 12 western counties in New York State:[citation needed] Allegany[citation needed], Cattaraugus[citation needed], Chautauqua[citation needed], Erie[citation needed], Genesee, Orleans, Niagara[citation needed], Wyoming[citation needed], Monroe[citation needed], Wayne[citation needed], Livingston and Ontario[citation needed], with a land area of 8,973 square miles (23,240 km2)[citation needed].

Compare the 11 [citation needed] notations in this single sentence about the counties of Western New York, (an entirely real place populated by real people), with the entry for Shire (Middle Earth), which outlines the four farthings of the fictional region that Tolkien's fictional Hobbits lived in, detailing areas such as Rushock Bog, the Overbourne Marshes, and the village of Hardbottle using 43 separate citations and not a single [citation needed].

And don't even get us started on the Sackville fucking Bagginses.

https://en.wikipedia.org/wiki/Western_New_York

Hungry ghost

Possibly the worst thing about "Hungry Ghosts" is that they always come back for more.

The second worst thing about "Hungry Ghosts" is that what they're coming back for more of is noisy sex with your dog.

http://en.wikipedia.org/wiki/Hungry_ghost

Hooked Bear

Fishing Season has begun. J. Audubon Woodlore goes in a boat and gets fishes. Here's Humphrey the Bear playing with one fish. He uses a ruler to make fishes in sizes. Here's Humphrey the Bear playing with one fish. J. Audubon Woodlore gets more fish for fishing rods. Humphrey gets a fish bag, fishing rods, and a net. J. Audubon Woodlore takes them gets fish seeds to put in the water like soil. Humphrey's trying to eat the small fish but one fish jumps and Humphrey throws it. J. Audubon Woodlore makes a rainbow with fishes and Humphrey gets some fish with a small fish and J. Audubon Woodlore goes in a boat and uses a ruler and see if the fish is so small and hits Humphrey on the head and the boat scratches Humphrey's head and Humphrey gets the fish and a fish balloon pops. Humphrey stubs his toe and says, "Ow-ow-ow!" and J. Audubon Woodlore holds two buckets of fish then Humphrey gets the hat from under the boat. Humphrey goes deep with his hat on and a fin is heading toward the five people and they run away from Humphrey with his hat on and takes his hat off and collects the fish bags and carries them to the fishairplane and pours the fish in. He gets one fish and J. Audubon Woodlore has dressed as a pilot ready to take the flight and the fish fall and Humphrey stubs his toe from the closing and the fish fall but Humphrey tries to eat them and he falls. J. Audubon Woodlore receives a call on the telephone from his superior to see if he's still stocking the lake with fish. Ranger Woodlore told him he was, but was told to stop because Fishing Season ended the previous day. In shock J. Audubon Woodlore cuts everyone's fishing lines, chases other fishermen away and throws all the caught fish out of the bucket and yells, "Fishing Season's over!" and draws an X on the "Fishing Open" sign and flips it over to the "Hunting Season Now Open" and it has begun for Humphrey.

This cartoon sounds M. Night Shyamalan–esque in its vapidity, brainlessness, utter incoherence, and soul-deadening effects. Also, because it has a twist ending.

Caddyshack

The mistaking-a-chocolate bar-for-a-piece-of-excrement-in-the-pool scene was filmed at Coral Ridge Country Club in Fort Lauderdale, Florida.[citation needed]

This should not be confused with the mistaking-a-chocolate-bar-for-a-piece-of-excrement-in-the-pool scene in Kurosawa's Ikiru, which was filmed in Fort Myers.

Capital punishment in New Hampshire

Since 1734, twenty-four people have been executed, with the last execution carried out in 1939. Since 2008, there is one person, who is black, on "Death Row"; however, there is no execution chamber or gallows, and they are unlikely to be "lynched" by Governor John Lynch, but not because of the irony.

Say what you will about the dour, humorless Yankee soul, but at least their governors don't go around executing people ironically. The governors of New York and California probably do ironic executions all the time. "Pshya, I totally 'killed' that guy. I guess it was cool or whatever."

http://en.wikipedia.org/wiki/Capital_punishment_in_New_Hampshire

Angry mob

Michael Graham explains that although "expressing support for values like individual responsibility, personal liberty, and economic freedom" was once very common and not seen as being radical, today these actions makes one become part of an "extremist rabble". Despite America's long history in questioning authority through rallies and marches, in the modern era, specifically during Barack Obama's time in office, one's "loyalty…decency, [and] sanity" can become questioned through the same actions. Instead of being a revolutionary, one merely becomes part of an "angry mob". Although "the Obama elites and media sycophants often complain about the 'angry mob'", it is rare that the motivations behind the opposition are looked into and analyzed. After Republican Scott Brown won office, columnist Charles Krauthammer described the mindset of what he viewed as angry mob voters: "[they have an] inchoate, unthinkable lashing-out at whoever happens to be in power - even at your liberal betters who are forcing on you an agenda that you can't see is in your own interest".

The major stereotype surrounding angry mobs involves a farmer wielding a pitchfork.

> *We really thought this one had a chance. It's sort of like if Michelangelo got all the way to the end of his statue of David, then decided to put a cock ring on him.*

http://en.wikipedia.org/wiki/Angry_mob

King Hippo

He is an obese man from the fictional Hippo Island (Not hailing from the real, sub-Antarctic Hippo Island).

The inhabitants of the real subantarctic Hippo Island of course beheaded their king in the early 1800s in the famous Hippo Island Revolution, and are now ruled by the six obese members of the Hippo Island People's Central Political Directorate.

http://en.wikipedia.org/wiki/King_Hippo

Timeshare tour

If the Guide is Licensed, he/she will then give the Prospect the Retail Price of the particular unit that best seemed to fit the Prospect's needs. If he/she is not a licensed Agent, a Licensed Agent will now step in to present the price. The Prospective Buyer will then be given an incentive to "Buy Today"; usually in the form of a discounted price that will only be good "Today". If the reply is No, or "I'd like to think about it", the Guide will ask the Prospect to please talk to one of his managers before the Prospect leaves. It is at this moment, that the Prospective Buyer realizes that his/her Tour has actually just begun.

They say that sometimes, late at night, you can still hear the ghostly wails of Prospects who thought their Tour could last forever, and who waited too long to make a decision and had to go talk to the manager. Or maybe that's just the substandard plumbing in this shitty timeshare complex. Either way, best to stick close to your Guide, kids.

http://en.wikipedia.org/wiki/Timeshare_tour

List of unusual units of measurement

Half of a cord, sometimes called a yard, is a rough unit of measure used in the United States that is equal to the amount of wood that can be loaded into the back of a pick-up truck, a non-flatbed truck whose body creates a cargo area that ranges between 2 to 2.5 ft deep but whose volume is encroached by the truck's wheel wells. Pick-up trucks come in short bed (5ft), standard bed (6ft), and long bed (8ft). As such, when an individual buys fire wood, usually from another private individual who posts a sign or ad and not from a true business or store, the wood's cost becomes relative to the size of pick-up truck the buyer happens to be driving. However, while a roadside sign may post price per yard or half-cord, sometimes a seller will reduce the price for a buyer driving a smaller truck, but not always, saying: *"Everybody knows 'a yard'/'half a cord' is whatever you can fit in the back of your pick-up; take it or leave it."*

Once your real family tires of your highly specific, yet thoroughly uninteresting anecdote about the time you felt you got swindled buying firewood, you can always share with your anonymous Wikipedia family.

http://en.wikipedia.org/wiki/List_of_unusual_units_of_measurement

Placeholder name

The usage of "Hon" in the US South, between men and women, or between women and anyone, should not be mistaken as flirtation, sexist, or diminutive. Sometimes, when new visitors to the South are visibly taken aback, someone nearby may interject, "Best get used to it, 'cus y'all done crossed the Hon Line ways back", which comment may also be off-putting to Northerners who are not used to talking to strangers or having strangers talk to them out of a narrow course of normal business, and never so informally. In the US North, being spoken to by strangers using familiar placeholders for their unknown names, results in the user being seen as deranged, intoxicated, and/or vagrant; however, more latitude is generally given in the North if the stranger using this familiar placeholder speaks with a southern accent.

> *"OK, so evidently you guys are sick of my firewood story. Have I told you about the time I went down south and these crazy women started calling me..."*
>
> *"**Yes** dad! Dammit, you're so **lame**!!"*

http://en.wikipedia.org/wiki/Placeholder_name

Todd Bridges

In 1998, Todd Bridges and his brother James Bridges were credited with saving the life of a 51 year old paraplegic woman, Stella Kline. The woman nearly drowned when her wheelchair rolled into a lake while she was fishing. It was later decided that water and wheel chairs are a bad combination.

The American Wheelchair Council admitted that it probably should have made such an obvious declaration years ago, but to be honest, it wasn't even aware that the American Wheelchair Council existed or that Todd Bridges was not in prison.

Eye color

Eye colors can range from the most common color, brown, to the least common.

They say that if you ever say the name of the least common eye color aloud, everything you see will suddenly be that color, for the brief, ecstatic moment right before your mind tears in half and you descend into gibbering madness.

http://en.wikipedia.org/wiki/Eye_color

Jonathan Singletary Dunham

Notable descendents
·Barack Obama (1961-), 44th President of the United States
·Scott Trimble (1977-), location scout and location manager (Transformers, Star Trek, Iron Man 2)

> *Sure, it seems silly now to lump these two together as "notable," but if history teaches us anything, it's that our memories of political leaders fade quickly, while an artist lives forever. Trimble will specifically live forever in the special part of hell reserved for everyone involved in the* Transformers *film franchise.*

Parking chair

The practice is often most effective when accompanied by the threat or actual occurrence of a "look of consternation" from a vigilant, often elderly neighbor who "keeps watch" in their neighbor's absence.

"Yeah, man, just go ahead and park, not sure why that chair was there. Wait, what's that old dude looking at us like that for? It's like he's threatening us with AHHH AHHH AHH AHHH" [parkers' faces all melt off like Nazis at the end of Raiders of the Lost Ark]

http://en.wikipedia.org/wiki/Parking_chair

Pinky and the Brain

In the 2006 film Lady in the Water, Bryce Dallas Howard's character is a sea creature that is called a narf. It is unsure whether the term was inspired by Pinky and the Brain or is a coincidence.

*Though other items in the director's filmography seem to indicate it was definitely **not** a coincidence. Namely the neighboring farmer in Signs named "Faboo" and the guy who intentionally runs himself over with a lawn mower in The Happening named "Hello-o-o, Nurse!"*

Critics agree that naming a main character in a major motion picture after a catchphrase involuntarily exclaimed by a brain-addled mouse in a decade-and-a-half-old cartoon would have been one of the most dignified of Shyamalan's recent career decisions.

This concludes the M. Night Shyamalan bashing in this book.

http://en.wikipedia.org/wiki/Pinky_and_the_Brain

Sichuan pepper

Sichuan pepper leaves tingly sensation to the tongue which many sex writers from eastern civilization have described as next best thing to orgasm, both in men and women.[citation needed]

> The lack of a citation for this entry is another tragic result of Wikipedia's failure to attract editors who have experienced orgasm.

Social engineering (political science)

Prohibitions on murder, rape, suicide and littering are all policies aimed at discouraging undesirable behaviors.

Yes, at first glance it seems frivolous to lump littering in with these other serious topics. But the last we checked, it is the only one that our government employs a lovable mascot character to discourage children from doing. We feel that the Forest Service's silence on the first three issues speaks volumes about their twisted priorities. (The notorious murder enthusiast, rape dabbler, and suicide aficionado Woodsy Owl has sadly made his own controversial personal views quite clear in various interviews over the years.)

http://en.wikipedia.org/wiki/Social_engineering_(political_science)

Stephen Butterworth

He was a first-rate applied mathematician. He often solved problems that others had regarded as insoluble. For his successes, he employed judicious approximations, penetrating physical insight, ingenious experiments, and skillful use of models. He was a quiet and unassuming man. Nevertheless, his knowledge and advice were widely sought and readily offered. He was respected by his colleagues and revered by his subordinates.

At this point in time, the graduate student that Professor Butterworth was forcing to edit his Wikipedia page emailed the professor asking "The next sentence I have says 'He has a foot-long cock.' Is that really something you want on there?"

http://en.wikipedia.org/wiki/Stephen_Butterworth

Turkish Taffy

In 1972 Tootsie Roll Industries purchased the rights to Bonomo's Turkish Taffy. A number of web based stories recite the same misconception that by the mid 1980s Bonomo's Turkish Taffy was shelved by Tootsie Roll Industries due to lack of interest. In reality, shortly following aqcuisition, Tootsie Roll Industries changed the sixty-year old tried and true smack-it crack-it formula to a soft taffy. They dropped the name "Turkish Taffy", changed the ingredients, packaging, and shape. Eventually the product was named Soft and Chewy Tootsie Taffy. It was this product that Tootsie Roll Industries shelved.

Turkish Taffy Truthers are a small but feisty group of internet users whose goal is to use Wikipedia to pull the blinders off the eyes of the sheeple and expose the real workings of Tootsie Roll Industries, which a number of web-based stories have conspired to obfuscate. Also, to make the Obama birth certificate crazies and lizard people nutjobs seem like they have their priorities firmly in place.

http://en.wikipedia.org/wiki/Turkish_Taffy

Confetti

Confetti is commonly used at social gatherings such as parties, weddings, and Bar Mitzvahs but is considered taboo at funerals.

Man, we've clearly been going to the wrong bar mitzvahs. And the wrong funerals.

http://en.wikipedia.org/wiki/Confetti

Fake orgasm

It can also include giving verbal indications that orgasm occurred.

We're not really qualified to give relationship advice, but if your partner at any point says to you "Oh, hey, I had an orgasm, like, a while ago, so, um, you can stop what you're doing any time you want, don't go on all day on my account," you may be in for some rough times ahead.

http://en.wikipedia.org/wiki/Fake_orgasm

Motherfucker

The word is also commonly used as an expletive. For example if a person is told an incredible tale or description of an event they may respond with "Motherfucker" said slowly.

> *"I spent large portions of my adult life editing Wikipedia pages about profanity rather than forming meaningful bonds with other people."*
>
> *"Motherfucker..." (said slowly)*

Drunk dialing

"Drunk texting" is a related phenomenon, and potentially yet more embarrassing for the sender as, once the message is sent, it cannot be retrieved; the message will most likely be misspelled (due to being drunk), and it might be reviewed and shared among many.

Bone up on your spelling skills now, kids! Honestly, children would do much better in school if more subjects were framed in terms of "you need to master this or else you'll humiliate yourself as an adult, when you're blotto."

http://en.wikipedia.org/wiki/Drunk_dialing

Big Bertha (comics)

Big Bertha has the ability to make herself super strong and durable (to the point of being bullet-proof) by becoming extraordinarily obese. It is implied that she has greater control of this ability and can distribute her fat content to select areas (i.e. just her breasts or buttocks or other areas), becoming "every man's dream."[volume & issue needed] She can also purge most fat from her body to take on a slimmer appearance. However, the latter ability is not as surreptitious as the former, since she has to regurgitate the collected fat masses in order to retain her normal shape. This is graphically illustrated in GLA #2; a helpful aside from the narrator (fellow GLA member Squirrel Girl's squirrel colleague "Monkey Joe") points out that "bulimia is never funny". Where this mass comes from originally is not addressed.

In addition to her mutant powers, Ashley is also a skilled pilot of conventional jet aircraft.

> In a surprise upset, the award for Most Baffling Phrase in This Article ended up going to "squirrel colleague."

http://en.wikipedia.org/wiki/Big_Bertha_(comics)

Quilt

The following list summarizes most of the reasons a person might decide to make a quilt:
-Bedding
-Decoration
-Armoury (see Gambeson)
-Commemoration (e.g. the "Twentieth century Women of Faith" quilt on the Patchwork page)
-Education (e.g. a "Science" quilt or a Gardening" quilt)
-Campaigning
-Documenting events / social history, etc.
-Artistic expression
-Traditional gift

In our opinion, the fact that "revenge" is missing from this list completely invalidates it. How awesome would a revenge quilt be? Little old ladies of the world, please do not let this omission discourage you from making a revenge quilt! Smother those who wrong you and your grandchildren/cats with handcrafted patchwork!

http://en.wikipedia.org/wiki/Quilt

Evil laughter

In comic books, where supervillains utter such laughs, it is variously rendered as mwahahaha, muwhahaha, muahahaha, buahahaha bwuhuhuhaha, etc. (Compare with Ho ho ho). These words are also commonly used on internet Blogs, Bulletin board systems, and games. There, they are generally used when some form of victory is attained, or to indicate superiority over someone else. The words are often used as either interjections or less frequently, as nouns.

"Evil laughter" is a commonly used adjective in novels as by saying "Evil laughter filled the room" or something to that effect creates a brilliant mental sound that everyone can immediately recognize as evil. By saying someone's laugh is "evil" you can immediately conjure up a mental image of that person and little other description is needed. Anyone can imagine someone evil, so not describing them makes the book more vivid and relate more to the reader.

This concludes Professor Easton Ellis's guest lecture. Your regular Harvard MFA program will resume tomorrow. Class dismissed.

https://en.wikipedia.org/wiki/Evil_laughter

Trix (cereal)

The plight of the Trix Rabbit has drawn comparisons to Sisyphus, a Greek figure who was doomed to endlessly repeat a futile task.

> *Not even the terrible Greek gods were as profoundly dickish as the kids in those commercials, though. Zeus's immortal heart could eventually be moved to pity, but not those adorable little monsters. "Silly rabbit," they would say, not sorry at all, not even knowing what sorry meant. "Trix are for kids."*

http://en.wikipedia.org/wiki/Trix_(cereal)

Charles Bronson (prisoner)

On 12 November 2010, Bronson was involved in another incident in Wakefield prison's F Wing, when he stripped naked, covered himself in butter and attacked six guards. Covering himself with butter apparently made him harder to control.

Bronson actually covered himself because he believed he was the reincarnated spirit of the Igbo death god Ogbunabali and thought the viscosity of the butter would make it easier to absorb the souls of sinners. But just before the the post-prison-rampage press conference he got kind of embarrassed about how ridiculous this sounded and when someone asked him if he had covered himself with butter to make himself harder to control, he just ran with the suggestion.

http://en.wikipedia.org/wiki/Charles_Bronson_(prisoner)

Aristotle's views on women

Aristotle wrote extensively on his views of the nature of semen but seemed to struggle with the concept of what a woman actually was and how her body functioned.

This actually refers to AristotleDerpy69, a well-respected user on the My Little Pony fan fiction forums.

http://en.wikipedia.org/wiki/Aristotle's_views_on_women

Hide-and-seek

The last person found doesn't get any prize or reward but it is accepted that he or she has the best hiding place.

> *The only hide-and-seek reward greater than the silent approbation of your fellow players is to stay hidden forever, to die in the closet under the laundry, with your skeletal remains found decades later, then taken and buried under a grave marked BEST HIDING PLACE. But few achieve such heights of glory.*

http://en.wikipedia.org/wiki/Hide-and-seek

Pinocchio paradox

Growth is a characteristic of life that can be observed in a living organism at any time. Therefore, Pinocchio will be telling the truth when he says "my nose will grow now", since the cells in his nose will grow (by a little amount which cannot be observed by the naked eye).

However, Pinocchio is not alive, but a marionette.

Remember, if you see a paragraph of obvious nonsense on Wikipedia, don't just delete it! Instead, you need to add a smug, pointless sentence correcting it. Otherwise nobody will know that you were right!

http://en.wikipedia.org/wiki/Pinocchio_paradox

Stephanie Ashworth

Ashworth previously played in the bands Sandpit and Scared of Horses. She married bandmate/frontman Paul Dempsey. She was offered the place in Courtney Love's Hole but declined.

Much to the dismay of Dempsey, who had been dropping little hints that he'd be totally cool with it all week.

Face/Off

The names Castor and Pollux come from a pair of brothers inGreek mythology that make up the Gemini constellation. The story itself, most notably the hatred between Archer and Troy, is very similar to that of Hector and Achilles, who fought against each other in the Trojan War. Additional influences may have come from the fact that the Greek and Roman god of archery, Apollo, was closely related with the city of Troy. The Archer is also a constellation and is significant because The Archer is the Sagittarius constellation. Therefore, we have this clash between the Gemini Twins and Sagittarius... it's polar opposite. Ironically, Castor and Pollux were also chosen as names for police dogs in another 1997 film, the sci-fi/horror The Relic starring Tom Sizemore.

> Somehow, the wildly incorrect use of the word "ironically" here transforms this paragraph from a muddled mess into a masterpiece of Dadaist poetry. This is in and of itself ironic.

http://en.wikipedia.org/wiki/Face/Off

The Original House of Pies

Their original logo, pictured here, obviously referenced the symbol for Pi (3.14). Their new logo has been updated to more accurately reflect a slice being cut from the whole pie. This change has not been well received from some visitors, as the phrase that was once heard uttered from a guest, "So, what's that, like the international symbol for p…. Oh yeh, nevermind" doesn't hold nearly as much weight. That and the symbol looked more like strips of bacon, than the symbol for pi.

Despite all the confusion over the logo, their slogan has remained unchanged for years: The Original House of Pies—Where our designer, customers, and Wikipedia page editors are all apparently high as balls.

http://en.wikipedia.org/wiki/The_Original_House_of_Pies

Piledriver (sexual)

The sexual piledriver must be executed carefully to prevent injury.[citation needed]

The state of Texas got really careless when they executed Ron "The Sexual Piledriver" Grabowski. A deputy moved in too quickly when he flipped the switch on the electric chair and got a splinter from the wooden handle.

CLASSROOM ACTIVITIES:
Hey kids! We left it pretty ambiguous what Ron "The Sexual Piledriver" Grabowski was being executed for, so why don't you draw us a picture of his mugshot! Be sure to list the litany of heinous crimes he no doubt committed, some of which may have earned him his cool nickname! The crimes don't have to be sexual in nature, the sex acts may have occurred after the crimes were technically committed. Quotes from tearful family members are not required, but will result in extra credit. Send your work to: info@citationneededbook.com

(Someone please actually do this.)

http://en.wikipedia.org/wiki/Piledriver_(sexual)

Stunt cock

The stunt cock is used in an extreme close up so as not to identify its bearer, the goal being to deceive the viewer into thinking that the stunt cock is actually the penis of the main actor. Thus a stunt cock is analogous to a "stunt man," who anonymously does dangerous live action sequences in place of the main actor. However, a stunt cock seldom performs dangerous acts on film.

At least they seldom do ever since the Stunt Cocks Local 542 worked a "no sexual piledrivers" clause into their last contract.

Knock Off (film)

Ray and Hendricks then learn that these knock off jeans are laden with nanobombs, which were developed by former KGB operatives who are in league with international terrorists that are utilizing a Russian Mafia's scheme to bring this deadly technology to the black market and extort $100,000,000.00 in monthly revenue from the world super powers. This particular order is to be shipped to the U.S. Also, we learn that Ting (soft drink) is a beverage.

Furthermore, we discover that the CIA head-quarters, in Hong Kong, is located on Lantau Island inside a huge Buddha statue. THEY WERE NANOBOMBS!, but in the end, Hong Kong is safe and so is the rest of the world.

> *Whether it's a cheesy Van Damme movie, your wedding vows, or the obituary of a noted philanthropist, there are very few things that cannot be improved with an all-caps THEY WERE NANOBOMBS! inserted at random. Except maybe a trip through airport security. Stick to just informing people that Ting is a beverage at airport security.*

http://en.wikipedia.org/wiki/Knock_Off_(film)

Touch typing

It is even possible for a child to type up to 150 WPM, although no news or video sources could be found for this statement.

> We've got dozens of toddlers chained to computers, each under constant video surveillance, with automated recordings playing every few minutes telling them that they'll get to see mommy and daddy again if they'd only type words fast on the keyboard. We'll get back to you when we have some answers.

http://en.wikipedia.org/wiki/Touch_typing

Black Gold (song)

The meaning of the song has been the topic of many debates. Some fans state that it simply is about racism and/or black soldiers fighting in a war ("You're a black soldier, white fight"). Other disagree and claim it is about the greed for oil (Black Gold is another term for oil). One other theory maintains that it is about the Gulf War and the obvious references to the Persian Gulf in the music video supports this theory. Dave Pirner is shown in the reflection of a pool which mirrors the shape of the Persian Gulf. Many lyrics from the song do match this idea. The lyrics "Two boys on a playground/trying to push each other down" could possibly mean the USA and Iraq fighting over "Black Gold". It has been theorized that the lines "Keeps the kids off the streets/gives 'em something to do, something to eat" could mean young men and women ("kids") joining the military.

And there is the fact that at about 1:56 various noises are heard: ambulance sirens, screams, cries, and what appears to be a news cast, which could represent the war. Pirner himself stated that the song was about war at the Dogwood Festival in Fayetteville, NC on April 24th, 2010. He also stated that he was against war.

Pirner then stated that he was mainly against war because "it reminds me of that crappy Soul Asylum song." He was not invited back to the Dogwood Festival in 2011.

http://en.wikipedia.org/wiki/Black_Gold_(song)

Coming of age

In the United States, Mexico and in Canada, when a child reaches the age of 16 he or she is allowed to drive and sometimes receives the responsibility of owning their own car. Girls' 16th Birthdays are traditionally called Sweet Sixteens. Depending on the family's religion or family background, there may be a ceremony signifying their coming of age. Some parents are very good about teaching their children the mysteries of life and proper values, whereas others let the schools and experience handle that for them, and many discover life's values through music.

Are teenagers still discovering life's values through Boston's "More Than A Feeling"? Love that fuckin' song, man. Dannh dannh de dant dannh, DANNH DANNNH, de dant dannh... Where was I? Oh, yeah, don't get teen pregnant, kids.

http://en.wikipedia.org/wiki/Coming_of_age

My Brother the Pig

After dripping his frozen thing on some magic crystals, a boy named George is transformed into a pig.

OK, so you've managed to get your thing frozen, and then, adding insult to injury, your thing starts dripping. If your instinct is to wander over to some magic crystals and see what happens if you drip your thing on them instead of immediately getting the hell to a doctor so he can have a look at your thing, you deserve to be transformed into something that willingly sleeps in its own filth.

http://en.wikipedia.org/wiki/My_Brother_the_Pig

Executions of Cossacks in Lebedin

The Execution And this was an ordinary Menshikov Craft: the wheel, put on a stake, but the easiest, is happy toy, and hang their heads cut. Guilt them to seek recognition of their own, and to serve as a reliable means prepohvalnoe then the mystery - of torture, which dogma and still is known of this Russian proverb: do not stick Yangel, soul is not he shall take off, and tell the truth, and which was carried on with the utmost accuracy and the direction of the Catholic Code is, in other words: the degree and the order-batozhem, whip and shinoyu i.e. razzhennym iron, are led with the meekness and hesitation and slowness of body of a man who from the seething, welded together and sits. Passed one test enters the second, and who all of them could not stand it, they worshiped, for a true guilty and is led to execution.

Were affected in such a way as not prevozmogshih torture, to nine people, the number of these things, perhaps, increased, but, judging from the cemetery, excommunicated from the Christian and known as Getmantsev must conclude that buried them here is not enough. Reliability of events (in particular, the number of executions) is the subject of debate.

Really? There are debates about this? Frankly, we don't see how this article could have been any clearer.

http://en.wikipedia.org/wiki/Executions_of_Cossacks_in_Lebedin

She-Ra

Adora, having been trained by the Horde her entire life, assumes leadership of the Great Rebellion. The epic battle to free Etheria from the grip of the Evil Horde rages on, spreading across the corners of the planet. Through this war, She-Ra calls upon her allies across the globe, using their special talents to battle against Horde creations.

Whether or not She-Ra and her forces were ever successful in defeating the Horde was never revealed as the series was short-lived.

We assume that if the series had been allowed to reach the conclusion its creators intended, the Evil Horde's eventual suppression of the rebellion and the unspeakable humanitarian atrocities they committed to ensure its demise would have been gruesomely depicted on pink lunchboxes and backpacks in elementary schools all across the country.

http://en.wikipedia.org/wiki/She-Ra

Talk:Seven minutes in heaven

Family Guy

Should this article mention the Family Guy episode that had the game in it?

Bumping Uglies?

Should the article clarify on what "bumping uglies" is?

Reality

Has anyone ever actually played this game? If so, how did it go?

> *We normally don't do talk pages, but this one just seemed to perfectly encapsulate the Wikipedia editing process:*
> *1) Can we wedge in a reference to Family Guy somehow?*
> *2) Let's very seriously discuss an obvious joke.*
> *3) What's sex like?*

About the Authors

Josh Fruhlinger is the creator of the Comics Curmudgeon, a surprisingly successful blog that makes fun of Mary Worth and Apartment 3-G and proves that pretty much anyone can become mildly famous on the Internet for any reason whatsoever, as long as they update every day. His writing has also appeared on Wonkette and The Awl, and his first novel, *The Enthusiast*, will be published in 2013. He lives in Baltimore with his wife Amber and his cat Hoagie.

Conor Lastowka is a writer for RiffTrax.com. His first novel, *Gone Whalin'*, will be published in 2013. He lives in San Diego with his wife Lauren and his cat Slidell. He is working on making his bio even more like Josh's.

Like what you've just read?

Be sure to check out Volume 1 on Amazon!

And follow us here for new entries daily:

Blog: citationneeded.tumblr.com

Podcast:

citationneeded.tumblr.com/thepodcast

(or search "citation needed" on iTunes)

Twitter: twitter.com/cit8tionneeded

Facebook: facebook.com/citationneeded

Made in the USA
Charleston, SC
19 August 2013